The Book of
LULWORTH

RODNEY LEGG

HALSGROVE

First published in Great Britain in 2002

This book is dedicated to the memory of
BRIAN O'HARE,
who died during its production.

Frontispiece photograph: *From Dungy Head, westwards to*
St Oswald's Bay, Man o' War Cove, Durdle Door, Swyre Head,
Bat's Head and White Nothe.

British Library Cataloguing-in-Publication Data
A CIP record for this title is available from the British Library

ISBN 1 84114 141 0

HALSGROVE

Halsgrove House
Lower Moor Way
Tiverton, Devon EX16 6SS
Tel: 01884 243242
Fax: 01884 243325
email: sales@halsgrove.com
website: www.halsgrove.com

Printed and bound in Great Britain by Bookcraft Ltd., Midsomer Norton

Whilst every care has been taken to ensure the accuracy of the
information contained in this book, the publisher disclaims responsibility
for any mistakes which may have been inadvertently included.

CONTENTS

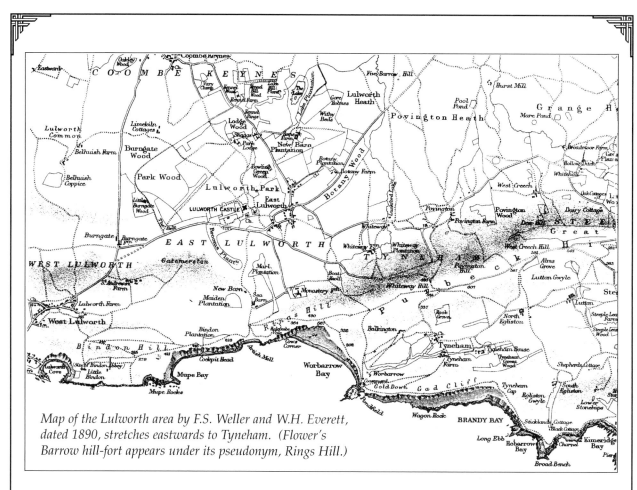

Map of the Lulworth area by F.S. Weller and W.H. Everett, dated 1890, stretches eastwards to Tyneham. (Flower's Barrow hill-fort appears under its pseudonym, Rings Hill.)

Durdle Door rock arch in profile, with a patchy sky, in an atmospheric study by Colin Graham, 1984.

INTRODUCTION

No one could have a more enjoyable assignment than writing about Lulworth. (Although even in the middle of Dorset's holiday coast, there are places that do not have a reliable supply of banana ice-cream.) Lulworth and its cliffs have been my stamping ground from cot-days onwards when home was in Bournemouth. Family picnics were followed by solitary visits as I hitchhiked, cycled, walked and climbed my way across Purbeck.

I went on to explore the Lulworth Ranges, through years of trespassing, but most of that is another story. Lulworth was for pleasure whereas Tyneham offered a cause. I've free-climbed much of the cliffs and declined the offer of a lift as a winchman dangled from a helicopter. If the opportunity arises again I'll take it. It is now a very different Lulworth from the 'silent hills between us and the Channel' described by East Lulworth vicar W.D. Filliter in 1908. At Lulworth those hills echo to the concussive thud of war and it has consequently become a much more exciting place. Perhaps that was its attraction to me as a teenage rebel. For although the initial reaction was outrage, at seeing tanks in the landscape, they also stirred boyish enthusiasm and pride and revived latent patriotism. I now cope dispassionately with the applied detachment of an historian.

The material generated by years of interviewing, both for magazine articles and books from about 1968 onwards, has been brought together here with another burst of visits and research. A recent find was Brian O'Hare, who sadly died before the publication of the book. He provided the detailed actuality of a Lulworth boy throughout the 1930s. It neatly fills the gap between my original clutch of old-timers and latter-day military manoeuvres.

Sergeant James O'Hare, of West Lulworth, whose nostalgic wartime verse appears in our introduction, in a caricature sketch of himself.

Brian's father, Jim O'Hare, went off to war as a Gunner, being Sergeant James O'Hare of the Royal Artillery. He never realised his ambition of producing a postcard of Lulworth Cove with the following verse, which now has its debut in print:

> *On Bindon Hill when day is done*
> *and slowly sinks the setting sun;*
> *o'er Portland's Isle then out of sight,*
> *when comes that welcome beam of light*
> *that guides the ships that pass at night,*
> *'tis then my vagrant thoughts do roam*
> *full many a mile from home sweet home.*
> *I think of Egypt and the Nile,*
> *of waves that wash a coral isle,*
> *of Afric' sun and desert sands,*
> *of wondrous scenes in other lands.*
> *But back to Hambury where winds caress,*
> *for on those alien shores there's emptiness.*
> *Just give me the rocks and wide rolling sea;*
> *the cliffs of dear Lulworth for ever for me.*
>
> *Then on to Durdle at break of day,*
> *blithely and gaily I wend my way,*
> *humming the tune of a well-known air,*
> *'over my shoulder' begone dull care.*
> *So take up your glasses and drink this toast:*
> *'Here's to the lovely Dorset coast,*
> *Here's to the rocks, the wide rolling sea,*
> *The cliffs of Lulworth for ever for me.'*

Our literary input has also benefited from new information about soldier poet Rupert Brooke and philosopher Bertrand Russell. Furthermore, in trawling through Thomas Hardy material I was delighted to read that an 87-year-old Herbert Weld was foremost among the last visitors noted in the author's own hand, in 1927. This reflects a personal hobby-horse of mine, as I jot down otherwise unrecorded place names to add to my large-scale maps of the county. Here is Hardy on just that – 'apropos of names left out of the Ordnance Map'.

The parish of Lulworth continues to yield rich pickings in terms of both places and personalities. It is hardly surprising that both then and now so many interested people are drawn to what has become known as the Jurassic coast. There's only one Lulworth Cove.

Sea spume and a deserted beach, looking south-eastwards from the inner curve of Lulworth Cove to Pepler's Point. Photographed by Colin Graham in 1982.

Left: *A paddle-steamer in the cove in the 1950s.*

Entrance to Lulworth Cove, seen from the south-west, showing the line of rocks from Stair Hole (foreground) to the Coastguard Lookout.

ACKNOWLEDGEMENTS

Very little of this book has come from published sources, my own included, and the only books on the table throughout its preparation have been the three bulky sections of the *Royal Commission on Historical Monument's County of Dorset (Volume Two, South-East)*, from 1970. Joan Berkeley's *Lulworth and the Welds*, published in 1971, has never been far away. Wilfrid Weld, the present head of the family, has kindly amplified and explained their complex genealogy.

My set of large-scale Ordnance Survey maps have been annotated over the years with local place names. This I mention in my introduction where I express delight at finding their omission was also one of Thomas Hardy's hobby-horses.

The bulk of the material existed in my own collection of letters, notes and cuttings. I systematically filtered them down – 'weeded' is the Whitehall term – into six almost manageable files. They include original jottings from school notebooks in 1960, which formed the basis of my *Purbeck Island* title in 1972. Additional material over the next two decades largely came either from readers of my journal, *Dorset – The County Magazine*, informants like Margaret Kraft, Rod Miller and Gerry Plant, and those met while out on the range. That for the purpose of this book is the Bindon Range of the Tank Gunnery School, of the Royal Armoured Corps, as I set aside most of the Tyneham story for another title.

There, as can happen in conflict, former adversaries have become friends for life. I was the first to praise the achievements of Major Mick Burgess as a double triumph for military ecology and public access. As a reformed character, which you have on the authority of General Sir Roy Redgrave, I no longer vandalise signs or trespass below the whiz of shells. Instead I receive my thrills at the bottom of an air-breaking stoop as a peregrine falcon falls on a racing pigeon and they break seawards almost co-joined. No score, this time, but a circle of fresh-strewn feathers by the path above Mupe Bay shows a different result.

The most recent contributions to my accumulation of memories came from Brian O'Hare, who died suddenly in 2002, after which his son Alwyn and brother Doug stepped into the breach to sort out various queries. They and others have provided additional photographs but the bulk are from the collection I have built up over the past four decades. John Ruston gave me the best Edwardian selection. These days many are my own but the superlative black and white landscape studies of semi-recent times must be those taken by Colin Graham before he left for Australia in 1985. For both of us it has been a pleasure to picture Lulworth and call it work.

Colin Graham's study of Man o' War Rocks, looking eastwards to the Pinion Rock and Dungy Head.

7

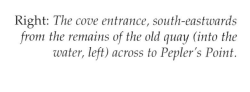

Left: *Arched view, looking due south into the English Channel, on a calm day in 1968.*

Right: *The inner curve of Lulworth Cove swarming with visitors in the hot summer of 1959, looking south-west from Bindon Hill to the Coastguard Lookout (left of centre).*

Chapter 1

CLASSIC JURASSIC COAST

That the incredible landform geology of the Lulworth coast now has international recognition is thanks to Steven Spielberg. *Jurassic Park* did for dinosaurs and their settings the reverse of what *Jaws* achieved for sharks. Extinction has a way of rendering safe even the most fearsome wildlife. Lulworth abounds in gems of landform geology, and is now at the heart of a World Heritage Site, with the ultimate accolade being confirmed by the United Nations Education, Scientific, and Cultural Organisation after its World Heritage Committee met in Helsinki in December 2001.

The true treasures in terms of age, appearance and rarity are the Jurassic trees on the cliffs east of Lulworth Cove. The Fossil Forest comprises the boles of pine-like and fern-like trees which rotted down and filled with sediment to form stone stumps that are now between two and three metres in diameter. A dozen of these gymnosperm moulds are set in a line on a rocky ledge above the waves, on strata tilted landward. The angle at which they stand is a direct result of the collision of continents, as tectonic plates impacted. They were once swamp trees growing beside the warm waters of 135 million years ago. No longer vertical, they tilt with the strata at about 40 degrees towards the cliff top. One pair grew only three metres apart.

Vertical landforms otherwise steal the show. West Lulworth parish begins in the west between Bat's Head, a perforated chalk cliff with the offshore stack of Butter Rock, and the world-famous rock arch of Durdle Door. This site has also been called Old Harry by a tabloid newspaper, which captioned its photograph. John Pitfield sent me this cutting and I reprinted it as a joke, much to the consternation of Dorset readers, who thought I should know the difference.

The rock arch dominates both the physical geology and the landscape of the mind. It is a symbol of Lulworth, Dorset and the World Heritage Site. Its existence is a result of a line of hard, upturned Portland stone standing seaward of much softer chalk cliffs. On either side of the outcrop the sea has broken through, across ribbons of rock, to create a wide shingle beach to the west and St Oswald's Bay and its inner Man o' War Cove on the east side. Here, just above sea level, there is a vein of Purbeck marble in the formation. Colours in the water are among the strongest on the Dorset coast, ranging from glorious turquoise to ultramarine, with Pinion Rock at the east end and Man o' War Rock defending its own inner cove in the opposite corner, against turbulence and the tidal currents.

Geology explained. This Victorian print shows the strata beside Stair Hole and Lulworth Cove beyond in a view eastwards to St Alban's Head.

Durdle Door as a name has the same origin as the arched Thurlstone off the Devon coast. Both derive from the Old English 'thyrel' or 'thirl' meaning holed. Initial 'th' sounds invariably render as 'd' in the Dorset dialect. 'Door' became a descriptive appendage once the original meaning became obscure. It is a hole that is only open to southerly gales, which are comparatively rare, and totally protected from winds and water to the north, east and due west. The little bay that is developing behind, in slow motion, is the result of south-westerlies which tend to be the most dynamic and prevailing weather systems in western counties. Even these are pushing into a cul-de-sac and erosion towards Newlands Warren is slower than that on the other side of the projecting bastion of stone.

Here, above Man o' War Cove, chalk often falls in quantity and gives St Oswald's Bay a milky streak into the open sea. In rough weather the Man o' War Rock gives the impression of a large warship ploughing through the waves. Stone-fronted cliffs resume between Dungy Head and Stair Hole and extend eastwards for two kilometres to Mupe Rocks where they jut into the immensity of Worbarrow Bay.

There are two breaches. Stair Hole is the setting for a West Lulworth geology lesson. The bowl-shaped depression above the rocks can act as a sound-box. Almost any time of the year, December and January included though perhaps not Christmas Day, you are liable to hear a teacher shouting its meaning to an impatient herd. Basically it goes like this. Lulworth is the best example in Britain of different rates of coastal erosion. An arm to the west points in the general direction of the magnificent sea-arch at Durdle Door, which for many is a walk too far. Below, at sea level in Stair Hole, there is a gash and a series of mini arches which show how the sea's break-through progresses, from cracks to gashes in the limestone wall, to the creation behind of a tiny bay. Here the next Lulworth Cove is in the making. The other wave of the hand is eastwards, to draw your attention to the tilted and twisted strata of the 'Lulworth Crumple' which is now explained as the physical effect from shock waves along the tectonic plates as continents collided. Harder layers of Portland stone rucked up the Middle and Upper Purbeck beds.

Further east, beyond the last grassy rise, Lulworth Cove is heralded as the erosion process brought to perfection. Soft layers of colourful Wealden sands have been scooped out in a semi-landlocked bay of table tennis-bat shape. Initial breaks of the Stair Hole sort have expanded into a wide opening through the ridge of Purbeck-Portland rocks. On the inland side the cliffs are sheer chalk. The little hamlet is an extension of West Lulworth village which follows the stream to the north-west extremity of the cove.

Inland, the Lulworth hills are rounded Hambury Tout, and the very different ridge-like Bindon Hill. Hambury Tout is topped at 454 feet with a Bronze-Age burial mound and has a name of some antiquity. Hambury means high barrow and tout was a lookout. William Lisle Bowles observed in his *Dissertation on the Celtic Deity Teutes*, in 1828, that 'most of the hills of the sea-coast, and through Dorsetshire, are still pronounced Teuts [toots] by the common people.'

East Lulworth ends with the Cretaceous period writ large. The scenic gap in the chalk cliffs at Arish Mell is dominated to the west by Cockpit Head and to the east by the entrenchments of Flower's Barrow hill-fort topping 550-feet sea cliffs above Worbarrow Bay. Because it is inside the Lulworth Ranges, then a no-go area, it was chosen in 1957 as the site for the outfall from the waste-water pipe from the Atomic Energy Establishment on Winfrith Heath. This was done as a precaution, in case of radioactive discharges. Fortunately we survived the first nuclear half-century without joining the dinosaurs.

Bat's Head

Western seaboard of West Lulworth parish, looking eastwards from Butter Rock to the Durdle Door outcrop.

Chalk cliffs westwards from Durdle Door to vertical Swyre Head and projecting Bat's Head.

Durdle Door

Above: *Durdle Door and its bay with Bull Rock, the offshore blob in Colin Graham's picture.*

Right: *View westwards along the top of Durdle Door. Offshore is Bull Rock, with Bat's Head projecting (top right).*

Left: *Cave view, from a hole in the cliff looking south-east towards Durdle Door.*

Man o' War Cove

Above: *Man o' War Cove with St Oswald's Bay beyond. Photographed by Colin Graham in 1984.*

Left: *Edwardian ladies with parasol on the bathing beach beside Man o' War Cove.*

Right: *The rocks of Man o' War Cove, comprising Man o' War Rock, the Norman Rock, and Pinion Rock off Dungy Head, in a view looking east from the Durdle Door outcrop.*

Below: *Man o' War Rock and Man o' War Cove, with an Edwardian yacht, looking south-westwards from the beach.*

Stair Hole

Left: *Rock-pool portraiture, looking seawards through the arch at Stair Hole.*

Right: *Geology lesson in the rocks, with Colin Graham's study of the 'Lulworth Crumple'.*

Stair Hole and the embryonic cove behind it, looking west towards Dungy Head.

Stair Hole

Above: *Closer view of Stair Hole and visitors. Photographed by Colin Graham in 1984.*

Right: *The line of rocks from Stair Hole to the Lookout above Lulworth Cove, from the west.*

Lulworth Cove

Left: *Across the cove, east to Little Bindon in about 1895, before the making of Britwell Drive in the foreground.*

Unusually empty, Lulworth Cove seen southwards from the beach to the entrance, with Pepler's Point on the far left.

Right: *The first car park at the cove was much nearer the sea (centre foreground).*

Lulworth Cove

Above: *Aerial view from the 1930s, westwards from Little Bindon, to Lulworth Cove hamlet (centre) and Britwell Drive (towards top left).*

Right: *The hamlet at Lulworth Cove, from the Coastguard Cottages (left) to the Post Office and Cove Hotel (right), looking south-west towards Britwell Drive in 1930.*

Left: *Covered charabanc, TR 6147 in Hants & Dorset livery, making a nostaligic return to Lulworth in 1984.*

Paddle-steamers

Left: *Arrival at Lulworth; visitors stream down two steeply-angled planks.*

Right: *Cosens & Co. operated most of the paddle-steamers, from Weymouth, before and after the Second World War.*

Right: *Post-war return of a paddle-steamer to Lulworth. The rocks (centre, foreground) show the outline of the eighteenth-century pier.*

Left: *Classic view of an Edwardian lady and gentlemen on the western cliffs of the cove. The picture is set off with the backdrop of a vintage Victorian paddle-steamer.*

Paddle-steamers

Above: *A paddle-steamer reverses out stern first. Looking north-west from Pepler's Point in the final decade of regular paddle-steamer operations.*

Below, left: *This 1960s postcard reveals the paddle-steamer's departure point, east of centre towards Pepler's Point, looking south from Bindon Hill. The same picture was still sold decades later.*

Below: *Looking down from the cliffs as another load of Edwardian visitors stream ashore from a paddle-steamer.*

The scene from the air, showing a reversing paddle-steamer, looking north-west from above the western side of the cove.

Below: *An Edwardian view of the unloading process shows the overcrowding that was commonplace in pleasure boats before modern safety legislation.*

Fossil Forest

Above: *Edwardian view of two stumps in the Fossil Forest, looking south-eastwards along the ledge.*

Below: *One of the best of the cycad stumps, looking southwards.*

Fossil Forest

Left: *Looking directly downwards into the spray on rocks below, this is a classic shot, by Colin Graham in 1984, of a superbly preserved Fossil Forest specimen.*

Right: *Petrified forest floor, desolate but with occasional eroded fern-like boles, looking south-westwards into the waves with a glimpse of Portland on the horizon.*

Mupe Bay

Left: *Close-up detail of the biggest of Mupe Rocks with its partners extending eastwards.*

Another of Colin Graham's timeless pictures of the Lulworth coast, from 1984, looking east across the inner arm of Mupe Bay.

Right: *View from Flower's Barrow, looking south-westwards, to Cockpit Head, Mupe Bay and Portland in 1897.*

Arish Mell

Above: *View of Arish Mell Gap in 1897, with an iron steamship washed up on the beach.
Further west is Cockpit Head.*

Below: *Arish Mell Gap, looking eastwards from Cockpit Head to Flower's Barrow.
Photographed by Colin Graham during his 1984 walk along the Lulworth coast.*

Chapter 2

AN ANCIENT LANDSCAPE

Military star sign marker for the banks and barrows on Bindon Hill in a view eastwards to the next waves of prehistoric banks on Flower's Barrow (centre left).

Ancient monuments past and present grace the hills and heaths of the Lulworth parishes. They range from a stone circle (gone) and numerous burial mounds (surviving) to a linear defensive work and hill-fort (both surviving). More esoteric is a medieval maze (lost). They present a snapshot of ancient history.

The surviving Bronze-Age stone circle in the Isle of Purbeck, at the other end of the Purbeck Hills, stands in a wood beside the Studland road. There was a second Purbeck stone circle in a similar location on the edge of the heath at East Lulworth. It was recorded by the antiquary Charles Warne in his *Ancient Dorset*, in 1872; he says it stood 'within living memory between East Lulworth and Povington, but not a vestige of it remains.' His informant, the author John Fitzgerald Pennie, said the stones were taken away by a farmer named Bower and used by him for gateposts and a bridge over a stream.

Pennie lamented the lack of interest in their preservation, both by his fellow East Lulworth villagers and gentleman antiquaries, and claimed to have discovered 'the inauguration stone of Celtic Kings.' Whether this was part of the circle, or elsewhere, is not clear as he does not give us a proper location, because he doubts there are 'ten persons in the county who would not consider it unprofitable labour to step over ten straws to see it.'

No later information has been forthcoming, but on checking old maps I found the name of Rempstone Gate at a point midway between Lulworth and Whiteway, where the old county road crosses the parish boundary between East Lulworth and Tyneham. The name Rempstone is a remarkable coincidence because its only other occurrence in the Isle of Purbeck is at Rempstone Hall, the seat of the Calcraft and Ryder families near Corfe Castle, where the surviving stone circle is situated.

In the vicinity of Rempstone Gate there are ten Bronze-Age burial mounds. Cemeteries of round barrows are often found in association with stone circles. There is also Bower's Coppice, preserving the farmer's name, though I have hit a blank with the etymology of the Rempstone name. 'Irrelevant stones' was the closest I could come. The other odd fact was that the lost stone circle at Rempstone Gate, being recorded in 1872, pre-dated discovery of the other one near Rempstone Hall, which was first spotted by archaeologists in 1908.

Water Barrows and Ferny Barrows are a cluster of Bronze-Age burial mounds, now inside the Lulworth Ranges, south-east of East Lulworth. The two Water Barrows and Ferny Barrows, a bracken-covered pair, lie on the mixed soils between the heath and chalk ridge of the Purbeck Hills. Their names express the character of the topography. The larger of the Water Barrows is three metres high and surrounded by a deep-cut ditch that is now three metres wide and nearly a metre deep. It is water-filled in winter.

Nearby is Thorny Barrow but this has been virtually eaten by a sandpit. Boat Knoll is a 250-feet rise topped with a round barrow on the south side of the road between East Lulworth and Whiteway Hill. These barrows with topographical names tend to be prominent mounds in the vicinity of Saxon settlement areas. Therefore they tended to be noticed and given descriptive names. Some often appear in charters and chronicles because fixed features in the landscape came in useful as boundary markers and rendezvous points. Numerous other barrows, scattered across the uninviting remoteness of the heath, lack the dignity of a name.

Hambury Tout, meaning 'high barrow lookout', is topped by a substantial Bronze-Age bell barrow of sophisticated Wessex Culture form, dated to between 2100BC and 1500BC. Some 25 metres in diameter and over three metres high, it is the burial mound opened

Bronze-Age burial mounds, known as Water Barrows, seen from the south, with Army star signs to show their ancient monument status.

Right: *Bank, ditch and counterscarp bank (right) of the Iron-Age rampart along Bindon Hill, looking westwards to Hambury Tout.*

Western ramparts of Flower's Barrow hill-fort, looking south-westwards to Cockpit Head, which is almost invisible in the mist.

by John Milner and described in 1790. He found 'at Hambury Toote' a large pile of ashes beneath a central cairn of stones. Above this lay a contracted skeleton with an urn placed on its chest.

The perfectly round and sheltered inlet of Lulworth Cove, with a protected beach towards Little Bindon on the east side, was chosen as one of the first points of landfall by Iron-Age immigrants from France in 500BC. They ensured the security of the landing beach and the coastal plain behind it by entrenching the entire length of Bindon Hill with an earthwork, all the way from the slopes above the present cove hamlet eastwards to the great chalk cliffs at Cockpit Head. Including its western arm, turning towards Lulworth Cove, this Double Ditch as it is known, is three kilometres in length. The protected land to the south includes the west-facing eastern shore of the cove and an east-facing beach in Mupe Bay. Whether the wind came from the west or east there would be a sheltered landing-place for boats arriving from the Continent.

An excavation in 1950 revealed that the bank and outer ditch, with a lesser counterscarp bank, was built on a slight marking-out bank just a few inches high. The main mound of chalk rubble was faced by a palisade of vertical timbers with horizontal wood stacked behind it. Most of the chalk came from quarry-pits and was hauled up ramped revetments behind rather than in front of the bank.

Different gangs seem to have tackled each section. Given the size and length of the earthwork, the estimate of 60 men taking 16 days to build the structure seems wildly optimistic considering the extent and effort involved.

Later more sophisticated hill-forts are a speciality of Dorset archaeology but they are a rarity in Purbeck. The one and only example, however, is a masterpiece of Iron-Age expertise and engineering. Flower's Barrow, at the western end of the Purbeck Hills, looms above Arish Mell and Worbarrow Bay and takes full advantage of the crumbling 565-feet chalk cliffs.

Sheep topping the northern bank of Flower's Barrow in a view westwards into the Bindon Range.

25

The fort encloses only four acres but it is likely that half as much again has 'gone off to sea' as the Lulworth fishermen would say. On the eastern, northern and western sides are double banks with ditches. The distances between the two lines of defences widen at the west and east ends because they were designed for the practicalities of slingstone warfare. Through effective defending, the aim was to keep an advantage of height over distance. The outer rampart had to be kept within firing range of the inner defences. In addition, because the attackers were firing upwards, however, their sling-shot would fall short and fail to hit the defending warriors. On the eastern side the inner rampart stands ten metres higher than its ditch and two metres higher than the top of the outer bank. The height advantage that comes with a steep slope enabled the builders to run the northern ramparts much closer together.

Small-scale excavations in 1939 revealed several slingstones. These were the standard form of defence in the complex fortifications of the Durotrigic peoples in the decades before the Roman invasion. On the domestic side the excavators explored a grain storage pit that had later been filled with refuse. Other undulations are probably the sites of huts. The original entrance is on the east side, along the ridgeway from Whiteway Hill, where the natural fall of the hill presents a passage overlooked by the outer rampart as the only easy approach. Both ramparts are slightly turned inwards to protect their double gateways.

Whatever tribal conflict Flower's Barrow may have seen, there can be little doubt as to its ultimate fate, when Vespasian's Second Legion, Augusta, stormed its way through the West Country after the Claudian landings of AD43. The position of a skeleton found on a rampart suggests a hasty burial after a battle in which the fort had fallen.

Hill-fort interior, above Worbarrow Bay, with the prehistoric surface slipping towards it.

J.F. Pennie, in his *Tale of a Modern Genius*, writes:

... a shepherding boy, while tending his flock on this hill, discovered lying just beneath the surface of the inner rampart a perfect skeleton of great stature (seven feet nine inches in length). It was placed with the head to the west; the skull not lying in line with the rest of the bones, but being found in an upright position, led to the conjecture that the warrior to whom it belonged had been decapitated. It was very perfect and the teeth beautifully white.

The height may be overstated as skeletons appear taller than their body was in life. Joints come apart and make measurements misleading. Evidence of brutal assaults, probably followed by massacres, have been found from Maiden Castle, Badbury Rings and Spetisbury Rings. Hod Hill was surrendered as a result of a siege. Ballista bolt artillery pieces had bombarded thatched huts with blazing projectiles. Fearsome iron bolts have been found embedded in vertebrae and skulls.

Field find from near Lulworth of a Romano-British peacock brooch, one of the earliest depictions of this unmistakable bird, which was valued as fine food as well as for its decorative uses.

Early Settlements

Above: *Eastern entrance of Flower's Barrow, looking westwards into the hill-fort in 1969.*

Below: *The view north-westwards from Rings Hill to Monastery Farm (bottom left) and Lulworth Castle (glimpsed at centre of left-hand woods).*

Little Bindon recycled stone from the original Bindon Abbey.
Looking north-westwards to Bindon Hill.

Lulworth, a Saxon name, means 'the manor or place of Lulla' and appears in the Domesday Book of 1087 as 'Lulourde, Loloworde, or Lulvorde.' Norman possessors were the de Lulleworths. William de Lulleworth, who died in 1279, rented the manor of Lulworth from Hugh de Roche, who was granted it by King Edward I, in recognition of which he had to provide the 'free service of one knight.' This would be his son and heir Reginald de Roche.

In 1300, Reginald's son, William, granted the manor of East Lulworth to John de Novo Burgo and his wife, and their heirs in perpetuity, for the sum of 100 marks payable to Reginald, and 200 marks to William.

The Novo Burgo or Newburgh family, named for Castle de Novo Burgo in Normandy, came latterly from Powerstock, near Bridport, but actually descended from aristocratic Norman roots. Henry de Newburgh, born at Novo Burgo, was created 1st Earl of Warwick by

The grotesque corbel stone serves as a monastic reminder of the medieval origins of Little Bindon.

William the Conqueror. Robert Newburgh (died 1158) was given the manor of Winfrith by Henry I and the parish became Winfrith Newburgh. His son Roger Newburgh (died 1172) and wife Matilda, Countess of Sarum, founded Bindon Abbey.

This Cistercian community began by the sea, in the little valley on the east side of Lulworth Cove, on flat ground beneath the southern slope of Bindon Hill. It dates from about 1150 but has left little documentary record or physical remains as it was moved from there only two decades later, to an inland site at Wool, in 1172. The monks also took the name Bindon with them. The ruins of the second Bindon Abbey stand beside the River Frome.

The original location, crossed by the Army fence beside a gate and Army red flag No. 2, is shown as 'Site of Bindon Abbey' on a Victorian map but printings of Ordnance Survey plans at the start of the twenty-first century no longer acknowledge it. The ground is covered by rank grass and bramble scrub. Nearby, an isolated chapel-cum-cottage known as Little Bindon stands above a wild gully with a hill separating it from the sea. It dates from about 1250, was re-roofed around 1500, and has brick dressings that date back to the 1700s. Reset in the east wall, below the gable, are two twelfth-century carvings from the original abbey. The east part was the chapel, with a cottage at the other end, under the same roof.

The first 'mill of Lulworth' in 1234 may have been at Arish Mell, beside Worbarrow Bay, because at that date it would have been of the tidal sort, like that at Christchurch, rather than relying on fresh-water power. 'Mell' was rendered as 'Mill' throughout the Middle Ages.

However, the purest form of this now beautiful name is the version 'Arse Mill.' The first element is a topographical reference to the opening into the sea, appearing as a slit in cliffs, between the smooth buttock-like slopes of the chalk hills.

Another fascinating place name takes on special importance as the earliest documented mention to maze-making in Dorset. It is also early for Britain as a whole. The intriguing entry, dating from 1438, refers to 'furlang voc le Mase' at East Lulworth where place-name historian A.D. Mills has found a field named Maze in a document of 1664.

The Newburghs of Winfrith Newburgh and Lulworth flourished until 1514 when Roger Newburgh died. He left only one daughter, Christiane Newburgh, who married John Marney, son and heir of Lord Marney. John outlived Christiane, but not for long, and the property then went to their two young daughters, ten-year-old Catherine and eight-year-old Elizabeth.

Catherine Marney's first marriage was to George Radcliffe. Her second partner was Sir Thomas Poynings, descended from the ancient Baron Poynings line, from Sussex and Essex. He became a General in the English Army in France and was created 1st Baron Poynings of East Lulworth. Having taken advantage of the suppression of the monasteries by Henry VIII in 1539, by acquiring much of the land belonging to Bindon Abbey, he built Mount Poynings with recycled abbey stone, on the north side of what is now Burngate Farm.

A complicated and disputed succession ended with the lands passing to his brother, Sir Adrian Poynings, Governor of Portland in 1562. They then passed from him to his younger daughters who married two brothers, Edward and George Moore. By the reign of James I (which began in 1603) the lands had passed to George Goring who sold almost all the estates to Thomas Howard, Earl of Sussex (died 1626).

An earlier Thomas Howard (died 1582) had already established a branch of the family at Lulworth. Having married Elizabeth Marney, sister of Lady Poynings, he was created 1st Viscount Bindon in 1559. The next Thomas Howard died without leaving any children and the property passed to Thomas Howard, Earl of Sussex, consolidating his hold of the area. He returns to our pages with the story of Lulworth Castle and that of Lulworth and the Welds.

St Andrew's Farm, a seventeenth-century house, barn and cottage within the confines of Lulworth Camp, perpetuates a link with a vanished chapel. Large-scale Ordnance Survey maps show the 'Site of St Andrew's Chapel' immediately west of the closest Army building on the north side of the farm. The latter is 'on site of Manor House.' St Andrew's Chapel, described as a 'capital' building, was built as a private family mausoleum by Thomas Howard, 3rd Viscount Bindon. Before the chapel gave it a new name the house was known as Tanders. Strip field cultivation from the Middle Ages has left south-facing hillside terraces above The Lanches and West Road in West Lulworth.

Cockpit Head and the beach at Arish Mell in an Edwardian view, looking south-westwards to Mupe Bay (far left).

Arish Mell (left) and Worbarrow Bay, in 1930, looking eastwards to St Alban's Head (top right).

The Old Mill at Lulworth Cove is now under the site of the pumping station. It was remembered as being a long, low thatched building with a steeply pitched thatched roof and sea-facing veranda. The whole building was covered in Virginia creeper, which became a mass of vivid crimson when seen from the cove in autumn sunsets.

'It was a proper artist's picture,' an old lady told me in 1968. She mentioned that Alfred Downing Fripp, a member of the Royal Society of Painters in Water Colours, painted the mill in her grandmother's time:

It used to hang over his son's fireplace, the home of the King's surgeon Sir Alfred Downing Fripp, in Portland Place. The picture came back to West Lulworth when Sir Alfred retired.

Other notables in that long line of painters include Sir John Everett Millais whose 'Departure of the Romans from Britain' is set in St Oswald's Bay, a rather unlikely point of embarkation. The surrealist painter Paul Nash with his petrified 'Stone Forest' should also be included in this list.

Chapter 3

LEGEND & LORE

Dorset villagers attacking a witch, in one of the illustrations for an exhibition to launch the Women's Institute folklore project, at West Lulworth.

The spectre of a Phantom Army haunts the western end of the Purbeck Hills inside what are now the Lulworth Ranges. East Lulworth folklore claims it for Flower's Barrow hill-fort, while West Lulworth spinster sisters Joan and Poppy Loader, collecting folklore for West Lulworth Women's Institute in 1932, place it on Bindon Hill. Its origin, in both accounts, is a landing in Lulworth Cove and tradition says it comprises a Roman legion.

The momentous historic sighting, which caused national consternation, was in December 1678 when Captain John Lawrence of Creech Grange, Steeple, in the company of his brother and four clay-cutters, were astounded to see a hostile army of massive proportions marching along the top of the ridge, above Tyneham, from Flower's Barrow to Whiteway Hill. The captain and his party fled to Wareham 'with all despatch' to raise the alarm. Lawrence went on to London where he deposed the particulars on oath.

He described a force of several thousand armed men. In preparation to meet them, 300 militia were quickly marshalled in Wareham. The medieval humped South Bridge over the River Frome was hastily barricaded. Scouts were sent to reconnoitre the coast. They found no trace of any hostile force nor evidence of a mass movement of men. All this was to the extreme embarrassment of Captain Lawrence but his acknowledged sincerity and loyalty saved him from reprimand or worse.

The Phantom Army, as it has been known, is held to presage a war, even though the first recorded occurrence in 1678 was seven years ahead of the Duke of Monmouth's rebellion and a decade away from the arrival of William of Orange to dethrone the Stuart monarchy.

Subsequent claims of sightings and soundings have included 'indistinct forms' as the fog drifts in from the sea to the accompaniment of 'the trampling

The Castle Inn, seen with a cart beside the sign in the 1920s, was the setting for 'corpse candle' phenomena in late-Victorian times.

of horses.' On such nights, according to the Loader ladies, 'no rabbits run and no dog will go near.'

The Loader sisters also record a ghost between the Yewleaze, on the site of Lulworth Camp, and the park wall of Lulworth Castle, which returns later in this book to scare the O'Hare children. It is the spectre of a murdered woman whose body was dragged to Needy Pit where her face was carved on a stone in the wall and is 'still to be seen, much defaced by time and weather.'

Another tale concerns an old farmhouse. The liklihood is that this was St Andrew's Farm rather than Burngate Farm:

My great aunt had come from Ireland on a visit, and was staying in this house. From the room in which she was sleeping, a short flight of wide steps with a hand rail on the upper side, led up to a room on a higher level. Waking suddenly, she saw the door of this room gently opened, and an old gentleman with knee breeches, buckled shoes, and lace ruffles on his coat. He came down the stairs, one hand on the rail, and leading with the other, an old lady dressed in a stiff brocade gown, who tapped the steps with her high gold-headed stick, as she came down. They turned their heads and smiled at her as they passed her bed, crossed the room, and went out by another door. My aunt has told me this tale many times and fully believed in it until the day of her death.

When the Castle Inn in West Lulworth was known as the Jolly Sailor, in the 1860s, landlord Thomas Winzar was a tight-fisted widower 'not at all prone to superstition.' He refused to let his daughter have her mother's 'big black chest' which lay 'at the foot of her big four-post bed.' Both knew that had been the mother's wish but the old man was adamant. Then, suddenly, his mood changed and he pleaded with her to take it. She reacted angrily and refused. The following morning he came to her in a state of terror and described 'corpse candles' that had appeared as a blue light dancing on the lid of the chest and across the bed. This time the daughter relented. The chest was carried to the daughter's home and the phenomenon stopped.

The Red Lion, the West Lulworth coaching inn which is now Churchfield House, also had its traditional apparition. She was the pretty young daughter of a former landlord who had met a tragic end. Her room was in use as a bedroom and she put in an appearance in front of a young male guest, who was staying at the seaside to improve his health, and woke to find the thin, pallid female figure beckoning him to follow her. He took this to be a premonition of his own death, which followed soon after.

I shall return later in the book to a more substantial and persistent legend, which claims Napoleon reconnoitred Lulworth Cove but abandoned plans to invade England, because it deserves deeper analysis.

Chapter 4

FISHING & SMUGGLING

Fishermen Bill Williams (seated) *and Joseph Miller with their pots and a granddaughter at Lulworth Cove, c.1900.*

Two age-old industries have been at the basis of local trade for centuries. One is a natural activity, gathering the produce of the sea; the other is man-made, being an automatic economic side-effect of taxation. For generations fishing and smuggling were synonymous in the Isle of Purbeck because fishermen and their boats provided the means for bringing contraband ashore.

In 1694 King William III presented Captain Peter Joliffe of Poole with a gold medal and chain in recognition of his boldness in attacking with his hoy a French privateer that was three times his strength. He had seen it capturing a Weymouth boat that was fishing the offshore Lulworth Grounds. Joliffe not only forced the enemy to release the captured boat but also caused the privateer to beach near Lulworth where local people took the crew prisoner.

Issue 3,098 of the *London Gazette* records the inscription on the medal:

His Majesty's Gift as a reward to Peter Joliffe of Poole, for his good service against the enemy in retaking a ketch of Weymouth from a French privateer, and chasing the said privateer on shore near Lulworth in the Isle of Purbeck, where he was broken to pieces.

Others, however, met and traded with their French counterparts. Phillip Taylor, Collector of Customs at the port of Weymouth, wrote in despair to his superiors in 1718:

The smuggling traders in these parts are grown to such a head that they bid defiance to all Law and Government. They come very often in gangs of 60 to 100 men to the shore in disguise armed with swords, pistols, blunderbusses, carbines, and quarter-staffs, and not only carry off the goods they land in defiance of the officers, but beat, knock down and abuse whoever they meet in their way, so that travelling by

33

night near the coast and the peace of the country are becoming very precarious; and if an effectual Law be not speedily passed, nothing but a military force can support the officers in discharge of their duties.

Even the gentry were implicated. Phillip Taylor reported on 11 April 1719:

We have from Sunday last searched Lulworth Castle belonging to Mr Weld, a Roman Catholic, and many other suspect houses in East and West Lulworth. In the house of Edward Bagwell, a tenant of Mr Weld, we seized about four gallons of brandy and about 12 pounds of pepper, from whence we proceeded into the Isle of Purbeck and places adjacent where we seized one anchor of red wine and two anchors of vinegar. And knowing it is the constant practice of smugglers to carry their goods off the coast as soon as possible after landing, as Blackmore [Vale] is the most disaffected part of the county abounding with the greatest numbers of dangerous rogues, two whereof we hear were Thursday last committed for declaring themselves for the Pretender, and consequently a place very fit to be searched, we have accordingly narrowly searched several houses and there seized yesterday in the home of Jacob Fox two anchors of brandy.

Seawards from Lulworth Castle, at the far end of the second cove in Mupe Bay, is the Smugglers' Cave, as the map now calls it. Formerly known as Bacon Hole it is remarkable in having a false wall, more than two metres high, built across its back end. This wall encloses a chamber five metres wide by three metres deep. There were the remains of a door which could have been concealed by rocks. The main cave is 13 metres deep by eight metres wide.

On the cliff top above the Smugglers' Cave is the ruin of a small stone winch-house, three metres square, which had its doorway facing the cliff edge and open sea. A little further to the west is a wartime pillbox with crinkle-cut walls, resulting from its concrete being poured into corrugated shuttering. Both structures share a strategic view over Mupe Rocks and Worbarrow Bay.

In 1766 the Government increased the scope of smuggling when it banned the importation of foreign-made silk and velvet to placate British weavers. A year before, 50,000 marchers converged on Westminster, protesting that their trade was collapsing under overseas competition. Rioting and attacks on the houses of importers continued into the night and the outcome was a set of restrictions that gave smugglers a new job.

A correspondent to the *Gentleman's Magazine* in 1768 said that one West Country smuggler was cheating Customs of about £20,000 a year. By 1779 it was calculated by the authorities that 31 smuggling boats, of between 20 and 70 tons, each with

Boat and Edwardian boatman beside the entrance to the Smugglers' Cave at the back of Mupe Bay.

Edwardian fisherman, beached beside Durdle Door.

Smugglers landing, moving and relaxing with their kegs in a print of 1807.

crews of up to 20, were operating from the Dorset coast. These vessels were credited with having brought 163,000 gallons of spirits and 780,000 pounds of tea into Dorset – and then far inland, into the heart of the kingdom – over the previous three years.

Dorset was a big player in the smuggling stakes and only one other English county operated more boats. As for productivity, Dorset was put in third place in terms of quantities of spirits landing, and was fourth in the list for illicit imports of tea.

'Much must be doing on the Dorset coast,' the Board of Customs heard, cryptically, in 1822. 'Brandy is offered at Yeovil at 8 shillings a gallon.' Later the officials assessed that no duty was being paid on two-thirds of the tea and half the brandy being consumed in the country. Only an insignificant proportion of the trade was intercepted and seized. This amounted to about 2,000 hogsheads of spirits in Devon, Dorset and Hampshire in a year. That was estimated as a tenth of the total being brought across the English Channel into the three western counties.

Defiance often led to violence. A brief cliff-top disturbance ending in murder rated only the following short paragraph in a local newspaper in 1832:

An encounter at Lulworth between a Preventive Officer named Knight and his assistant and a party of smugglers resulted in the officer being thrown over the cliffs. He died soon after being found.

The story is told in more detail on a gravestone from Weymouth's Bury Street cemetery, now in the town museum:

Sacred to the Memory of Lieutenant Thomas Edward Knight, RN, of Folkestone, Kent, Aged 42, who in the execution of his duty as the Chief Officer of the Coastguard was wantonly attacked by a body of smugglers near Lulworth on the night of 28th of June, 1832, by whom after being unmercifully beaten he was thrown over the cliff near Durdle Door from the effects of which he died the following day. By his untimely death the public service has lost a valuable and universally respected officer and sincere friend and his wife and family an affectionate husband and father.

That memorial dates from the closing years of the smuggling era. Two centuries of heavy taxation on spirits had brought prosperity to those in a position to evade the Excise – the fishermen of the South Coast and those in the manorial homes who financed the illicit cargoes – with the gamble being on the past success rate continuing. Cargoes being smuggled into England along the sparsely inhabited shore between Osmington and Worbarrow Bay were particularly lucrative as they could be sent inland with little hindrance, whereas those goods smuggled in to Portland and Purbeck faced a second shipment, across harbours, to reach their final markets beyond.

The coast west of Lulworth, inland from Ringstead Bay, features in Thomas Hardy's smuggling tale, *The Distracted Preacher*, published in 1879. More revealing than anything he put into print, however, are these jottings from the author's notebook, dated 22 March 1871:

While superintending the church music (from 1801 onwards to about 1805) my grandfather used to do a little in smuggling, his house being a very lonely one, none of the others in Higher, or Upper, Bockhampton being then built, or only one other. He sometimes had as many as 80 tubs in a dark closet (afterwards destroyed in altering the staircase) – each tub containing four gallons. The spirits often smelt all over the house, being proof, and had to be lowered for drinking. The tubs, or little elongated barrels, were of thin staves with wooden hoops. (I remember one of them which had been turned into a bucket by knocking out one head and putting [on] a handle.) They were brought at night by men on horseback, 'slung', or in carts. A whiplash across the window-pane would wake my grandfather at two or three in the morning, and he would dress and go down. Not a soul was there, but a heap of tubs loomed up in front of the door. He would set to work and stow them away in the dark closet aforesaid, and nothing more would happen till dark the following evening, when groups of dark, long-bearded fellows would arrive, and carry off the tubs in twos and fours slung over their shoulders.

The last person I was able to interview with personal knowledge of the Lulworth smugglers was Walter Miller of Chaldon Herring, who was born on the Burning Cliff at Ringstead, on 24 June 1890. He also passed on advice received from Dorset essayist Llewelyn Powys who was living in the former Coastguard Cottages on White Nothe: 'If you see an old man, ask him all you can.' So I did just that and have done so ever since, though seldom with such rich results:

My grandfather, Joseph Miller, was born at Worbarrow. He died at West Lulworth in about 1911, aged about 78. All the Miller family were smugglers before the Crimean War. The landowners and gentry smiled at this as it wasn't considered a crime. If they were caught with their gear and their boat and all that, they had six months imprisonment but not hard labour.

One of my great uncles did his time at Dorchester. He was unlucky to be caught, and when he came out of gaol he was met by the squires and whatever and taken to the King's Arms for a good meal; because cellars were getting low, you see. They condoned it in a way.

We have a grapple, used to grapple up the barrels when they were sunk at the bottom. Grandfather, Joseph, had to give up smuggling in 1854 because the Russian War broke out and all the coastguards were called up to serve in the Baltic Fleet. Then they recruited all the smugglers to be Extra-men, as they called them; that is, [auxiliary] coastguards.

Old Harry Vye and my grandfather and a few more had to sit on the cliff and watch for the smugglers who didn't come! They couldn't risk doing the two jobs at once. That's George Begg [pointing at a

Beached boats and the cove boathouses in pre-café days, in 1905, with terraced lawns above.

Moonfleet, *John Meade Falkner's classic smuggling adventure being filmed by the BBC as* Smugglers' Bay, *on the Dorset coast in 1964.*

photograph]. He didn't like me; he used to think I was too mischief-full or something. There was a story of a coastguard who accused a smuggler of doing something, pulled out a revolver, and shot the man. What comforted the smugglers was that this coastguard was called up by the fleet to the Russian War, got frostbite – and both his ears fell off. They said it was retribution.

George Begg was at Ringstead and had a boat of his own and went to Cherbourg to get a load. He had a 22-foot lerret [Dorset rowing boat, pointed at both bow and stern] and built a house at Ringstead to conceal it. The boat wasn't on the beach. When he wanted he just had to slip it out and go to France.

He was a clever old fellow. He used to wear these white trousers when I was a boy. I suppose he died about 85 in 1898. Dr William Good, the surgeon and medical officer from Dorchester, came twice and he said it was finished, but George Begg got up and went to sea again. He had another bout and this time the doctor said: 'I think he will do.'

He died! Dr Good was wrong in all his predictions. 'No bloody good', we used to say about him. It didn't enhance my father's opinion of doctors.

Walter Miller went on to tell me how the old fishermen lived and worked by pot-fishing in the shallow offshore waters and across the Lulworth Grounds – called the Lulworth Banks on the Admiralty chart – which extend south-west towards Weymouth Bay. He saw a framed photograph of what I took to be a lobster and was corrected instantly, being told that it was a male crayfish. At least I hadn't called it a crab:

Lobsters used to be caught more than crabs, as those change their skins and are slim before they do so. The saying is that crabs are good when there is an 'r' in the month. But in May, June and July they aren't much good.

There were 15 fishermen at Lulworth, and now there's only two. There were around six at Worbarrow. There was Jack and Tom, and another called Tarry, and his mate, and then there was old Charlie. All were one family originally but Henry Miller, the last one, had two sons, Jack and Tom, and both died during the war after the occupation [of Tyneham by the Army in 1943].

At Ringstead the catch was rowed to Weymouth. That at Worbarrow was taken by the fishmongers who used to come down over Tyneham Hill from Wareham. They came the same to Lulworth. Father and them, when they couldn't come, carried their catch on their backs to Weymouth and that was never considered any trouble. The fishmongers at Wareham, when they had caught too much, put what was left over into a packing case. The lobsters were live, with seaweed over them. They put them on a fast passenger train to London and they were sold at Billingsgate.

When mother had two lobsters, a pound and a half, she would cook them, cool them down, put them in a bucket and I'd take them and sell them at 9 pence a pound. That made your mouth water! Everyone would have a feed of lobster sometimes. Good sirloin beef was then 8 pence a pound. Visitors would come down and get the lobsters fresh; cooked on spatches.

All these fishermen were rabbit catchers in the winter. They had to because you couldn't make a living out of fishing alone as you couldn't earn enough; there wasn't enough gear. Sixty pots was as much as you could do. Now they work 400 and the Lulworth Grounds, a huge triangular shape off Lulworth, is prime fishing. They come up from Swanage and down from Brixham. But the lobsters aren't there now and we consider it's over-fished. In the old days everything had a chance to live.

Mrs A. Moulder recorded a conversation with an elderly weather-beaten Lulworth lady which she sent to me in 1969:

Talking one day about fishing, she told me that since the coming of the [Tank] Gunnery School lobster fishing had been severely restricted. Many years before, there had also been flourishing, profitable oyster-beds. Oyster fishing was done on quite a large scale and an oyster pond was made on the west side of the cove, where the fish were kept till wanted. [She pointed to the outer wall of the pond, which could be seen at low water, though few people knew its origin.]

The old lady was one of the last to remember that a fair was held, on the former broad stone jetty at Lulworth Cove, each Easter Monday. The construction was washed away and the last fair stall was then pitched near the Cove Hotel. Charlie Miller and his son Dave were the resident lobster fishermen who put out to sea in the 1930s. Their pots were marked by cork buoys, painted red, and Charlie hauled them aboard with a boat-hook. Charlie nicked their claws, to prevent them tearing at each other, and put them in a floating keep-box on coming back into the cove. Not only were the local hotels and restaurants supplied but the paddle-steamers brought solid business.

Brian O'Hare, born at West Lulworth in 1929, was playing beside Lulworth Cove when he found himself captured for posterity in a way that hardly appealed to an eight-year-old boy. He was sitting beside the water, early one morning, as an elderly lady sat behind an easel. She was painting the scene and encouraged Brian to pose as a fisherman, with rolled-up trousers, as he displayed his prowess with a shrimp-net. At the end of his debut as a male model he asked for a reward and suggested a penny ice-cream as recompense. He was firmly told that the

Young Brian O'Hare posed on a rock at Lulworth Cove for artist Molly Brett and was dismayed to find that Enid Blyton's illustrator had turned him into a teddy bear.

completed painting, as a permanent record for the day, would be 'quite sufficient, even for such a forward boy.' Then he summoned up the courage to look at the work and was appalled at the affront to his dignity; he saw himself portrayed as a teddy bear. Later he found out that the artist was Molly Brett and that she was working as an illustrator for children's books written by Enid Blyton.

Beyond Durdle Door, dangling from the sheer cliff in the remote hollow at Scratchy Bottom, there was an iron chain. Shepherd's boy Clarence Ellis of Hambury Farm, who grew up around Newlands Warren, was sure that it was still being used by smugglers in the 1930s. Doug O'Hare, his best friend, believed that they used Bull Rock as an offshore marker in foggy weather. He talked of hearing people moving about at night, and found trampled grass and other signs of disturbance in the morning, but without any of the usual traces left by campers, fishermen or tramps.

Chapter 5

TWO PARISH CHURCHES

The villages of East Lulworth and West Lulworth have their own parish churches. The Anglican church at East Lulworth became distanced from its community; it was re-located eastwards, as parkland was created around Lulworth Castle. The church was also later upstaged, in terms both of the old religion and historical significance, when the Weld family built their own Catholic chapel in the grounds of the castle in 1786. The Anglican church, which still stands, is dedicated to St Andrew and dates back to pre-Reformation Catholic times and long pre-dates both the castle and the arrival of the Welds; it dates from around 1312.

As a building it has had its share of changes, with only the bold fifteenth-century tower surviving intact through both

Consecrated in 1787 the chapel in the grounds of Lulworth Castle was the first Roman Catholic church to be built in England after the Reformation of 1529.

major rebuildings of 1788 and 1864. It is supported at the corners by huge buttresses. Other fifteenth-century touches include an octagonal quatrefoil font, the west window, and springings which supported a stone-vaulted ceiling. During its Georgian rebuilding, in 1788, the church was given a semi-circular apse at the chancel end. It was probably 'of some distinction', says church historian Fred Pitfield from Bere Regis, because the architect and builder was John Tasker, who had just finished the nearby Catholic chapel. Both projects were financed by landowner Thomas Weld.

Once the apse had gone out of fashion, it was removed by the Victorians in 1863. It was dismissed as work of 'very mean

St Andrew's Church, with an embattled tower and pinnacles, at East Lulworth.

West Lulworth

Above: *Looking eastwards along Main Street towards the Castle Inn, this pen-and-wash drawing of 1862 shows the medieval Parish Church at West Lulworth shortly before demolition.*

Below: *The replacement West Lulworth Parish Church, with Vicarage to match, seen from the south-east in 1906.*

Lulworth Castle and East Lulworth Parish Church.
Photographed from the south-west, by Colin Graham on Bindon Hill in 1981.

character' with 'nothing of remembrance'. Young architect Thomas Hardy, working for John Hicks of Dorchester, drew up the new plans and the builders, Wellspring & Son, were also from the county town. The interesting aspect of the design is that they unwittingly resurrected the original medieval floor-plan. 'In clearing away the ground the foundations of the old chancel were discovered and the new one has been carried out to the same extent.'

The Parish Church at East Lulworth contains a memorial to wealthy William Baring MP who drowned at Lulworth on 19 July 1820. He was the fourth son of the eminent financier Sir Francis Baring (1740–1810).

West Lulworth has entirely lost its original church apart from its site and churchyard. This lies 100 metres east of the war memorial, on the north side of the Main Road, opposite Spindrift, No. 11 and the Old Bakery. A plaque records the significance of the small enclosure of grass and graves: 'The site of the old parish church, pre-Norman in foundation, demolished in 1869 when the present church was built.'

Certainly it was there in the thirteenth century, functioning as a chapelry of Winfrith, the next parish to the north. During the consecration of the replacement, in May 1870, the original roadside church was roundly condemned for:

... its dilapidated condition, and the awkward manner

in which the cottages on each side intruded upon precincts, unpleasantly disturbing the impression of sanctity, solemnity, and dignity that we are wont to associate with our ideas of a parish church.

Just inside the gate is the grave of Obadiah Legg of East Farm who died in 1912. To his left is a cross, beneath the yew tree, dedicated to several war heroes including Charles William Haime, killed at Salonika, and Arthur Edward Silverton RN, commander of HMS *Defiance*, who was lost when the armoured cruiser was blown up at the Battle of Jutland on 31 May 1916. To the right is a stone erected to the memory of Robert Dudgeon, aged 29, who was the cook aboard the *Avalanche*, which sank off Portland after colliding with the *Forest* in 1877.

As for the present Holy Trinity Parish Church, at the west end of West Road (which now tends to be called Church Street because of its presence), it will come back into our story for its connection with Thomas Hardy the architect. He was working in Dorchester as John Hicks' assistant. He continued there for the completion of the project, sorting out details after Hicks had died, before working for George Crickmay's practice in Weymouth. Wellspring & Son of Dorchester were the builders. The carving of the columns, and a scriptural text placed above the chancel arch, were the work of Benjamin Grassby, also from Dorchester, whose firm survives to this day.

As a result of being at the heart of the holiday coast, the newly-restored church soon found itself adopted by an acclaimed ecclesiastic friend, the Right Revd John Wordsworth (1843–1911). Although he was Bishop of Salisbury, from 1885 until his death, his trinity of addresses extended from The Palace, Salisbury, and Lollards' Tower, Lambeth, to a home at West Lulworth. His strong associations with Dorset included second wife Mary Williams, the daughter of Colonel Robert Williams MP from Bridehead, in the hills between Dorchester and Bridport. He was the authority on *The Law of the Church and Marriage with a Deceased Wife's Sister* and the author of many pieces of practical advice relating to ordination, scripture, *The Invocation of Saints and the 22nd Article*. A plaque in the chancel of Holy Trinity records that 'in these years he frequently ministered and worshipped here.'

Thomas Hardy the architect worked on plans for the replacement Holy Trinity in 1869.

Chapter 6

LULWORTH CASTLE

This striking bas-relief photograph taken by Brian Hunt in 1976 shows the eastern entrance steps.

The ruin of Lulworth Castle, a gutted shell since its fateful fire on 29 August 1929, represents a mock-fortification rather than a fortress. It was a product of the romantic imagination that was prominent during the decade after medieval chivalry had become the new nostalgia, as celebrated in Edmund Spenser's *Faerie Queene* (although his allegory of the cultural clash between Protestantism and Puritanism was coming to pass). Lacking in any defensive purpose it was nevertheless too useful a building to escape the clash between the next King and Parliament.

Pretty and picturesque, brick-built but faced in neat Portland ashlar, it could have been a neo-Gothic folly. In fact it pre-dates its appearance by a century and a half. Sir Thomas Poynings, who married Catherine Marney, bought the Bindon Abbey estate and built a substantial house between the two Lulworth villages. Mount Poynings,

constructed between 1541 and 1545, stood beside what is now Burngate Farm. The riches of Sir John Marney had passed to his daughters Elizabeth and Catherine. The latter died young, widowed and childless, and her money and Dorset lands, including Mount Poynings, passed to Elizabeth who married Thomas Howard, 1st Viscount Howard of Bindon (died 1582). He was the second son of the 3rd Duke of Norfolk. The title Viscount Bindon was created in 1555.

The title passed to their eldest son, Henry Howard, 2nd Viscount Howard of Bindon (died 1590). He was the black sheep of the family, about whom his father complained to the Privy Council, pleading that Henry's wife:

... be protected from the practices of him and of the naughty queen he keeps, she having been already beaten most pitifully and many ways else misused.

Engravings of the Castle

Above: *Eighteenth-century print of Lulworth Castle, looking south-west. It also shows East Lulworth Parish Church (the tower can be glimpsed, far left).*

Below: *Nineteenth-century J.M.W. Turner print of Lulworth Castle (right) and Parish Church (centre) looking westwards, inland towards the chalk downs.*

He seems to have been something of a pirate rather than a prospective castle builder.

Having died without leaving a son, the title passed to his brother, Thomas Howard, 3rd Viscount Howard of Bindon (died 1611). The land at Lulworth also passed to him, with the death in October 1600 of child heiress Ambrosia Gorges, who inherited the Bindon lands of her grandfather, Henry Howard. The 3rd Viscount moved into the old manor house, Bindon House, which was built in 1575 beside the ruins of Bindon Abbey. He is said to have built St Andrew's Chapel, at St Andrew's Farm, as the family mausoleum.

Mount Poynings stood just east of what is now the B3071, as it approaches Lulworth Camp from Wool. The precise point, on the 400-feet contour 100 metres north of the present Burngate Farm, is now an area of disturbed undulations. The original Burngate – meaning Brown Gate – was a grange of Bindon

Abbey, after it was moved from Lulworth Cove to Wool in 1172. Stone from Little Bindon, the original Bindon Abbey at the seaside, had been used by Sir Thomas Poynings to build his house.

Thomas Howard, 3rd Viscount Howard, decided to demolish Mount Poynings and replace it with a castle at East Lulworth with a view down the valley to the sea, through the Arish Mell Gap. Having been appointed Keeper of the Royal Game in Dorsetshire in 1603, he was responsible for the warren and chase of the Isle of Purbeck and obtained a royal licence to 'inclose and impark' 1,000 acres at East Lulworth in 1605. The date of the building was confirmed in 1968 when Miss Clare Talbot, archivist for the Marquess of Salisbury, discovered a letter received by his ancestor Robert Cecil, Earl of Salisbury, on 1 July 1608. Written by Thomas Howard, it contained a postscript telling Cecil he had given him the idea for building the new castle, a job he had recently started:

The Lake

Left: *Rhododendron time beside The Lake, looking northwards to the boathouse in 1900.*

Right: *Swans and cygnets on The Lake, making for the southern shore in 1900.*

Left: *Further south along The Lake, looking north-west into Lake Hill Plantation.*

Lulworth Castle

Left: *The north side of Lulworth Castle, looking south along the drive. Photographed by E. Dodshon in 1926.*

Right: *Bournemouth Natural Science Society, photographed from the south-west by E. Dodshon, on its visit to Lulworth Castle on 5 June 1926.*

Left: *The western steps formed the back exit from Lulworth Castle. Looking south-eastwards, a shuttered boudoir can be seen on the far right of the ground floor. Photographed by E. Dodshon, 1926.*

Right: *Pastoral view looking west across Lulworth Park, early in 1891, with trees growing either side of the eastern steps and an almost totally consumed haystack to the north (right).*

If the little pile in Lulworth Park shall prove pretty or worth the labour bestowed in the erecting of it, I will acknowledge as the truth is, that your lordship's powerful speech to me at Bindon to have laid the first foundation of the pile in my mind, which ever since hath laboured for a speedy finishing for contentment of those, whose further living of that place the care is taken.

Thomas Gerard, writing the *Survey of Dorsetshire* as Dorset's first book in the 1620s, tells us that Lulworth Castle is:

... a fine castle, mounted on high with turrets at each corner, well seated for prospect and pleasure; but of little other use, although it stands adjoining to the sea.

It is built on a square plan, with walls facing the four points of the compass, and a castellated round tower at each corner. County historian John Hutchins, who incorrectly gave 1588 as the starting date for the construction of the building, believes that the terrace around the castle was once known as 'The Cloisters' because it was paved with the stone that had been brought from the cloisters of Bindon Abbey (meaning Bindon at Wool not Bindon at Lulworth).

In order to finance this increasingly ambitious project, in April 1608, Thomas Howard, 3rd Viscount Bindon, may have agreed to part with lands beyond the park pale to his cousin, Lord Thomas Howard, 1st Earl of Suffolk and 1st Baron Howard de Walden (1561–1626). An itemised account for a week's work shows that 15 masons, including one named Codd, were the main contractors, with 60 other craftsmen and labourers being employed on a daily piece-work basis for the two-year project.

The 3rd Viscount built Lulworth Castle specifically to attract James I. Like the Cecil property of Cranborne Manor, it was designed as a lavish hunting lodge and was fit for a king – although the Viscount did not live to witness this very occurrence. He died in the spring of 1611 and his cousin reunited Lulworth Castle with its estate. James I was the first royal visitor, at the invitation of the Earl of Suffolk, also joint Lord-

James I made the first royal visit to Lulworth Castle.

Lieutenant of Dorsetshire and the 'town and county of Poole.' He invited James I for a hunting expedition which took place in 1615. The King was suffering 'swollen legs' and 'chose to disport himself in the park, as also in the Island of Purbeck near adjoining.'

Because Lulworth Castle was ahead of its time, it must have had a London architect, although the only attribution on the ground has been to mason and contractor William Arnold who 'drew a plot for Cranborne House' in 1610. The link between Lord Bindon and Robert Cecil make this very likely. Deft touches that fit his style include the broad flight of steps and the balustraded terrace, on the east side. The classical entrance was added to the castle later.

The Earl of Suffolk was a naval hero. To Elizabeth I he had been her 'good Thomas.' As a dashing young seaman he had led a squadron in the face of overwhelming odds against Spanish treasure ships off the Azores and ended the century as an admiral. He was created Earl of Suffolk on 21 July 1603.

In 1614 he gained further glory when he became Lord High Treasurer of England. He dedicated much of his time to building Audley End, his stately pile in Essex, to palatial proportions. However, in 1618, he experienced financial difficulties; he was accused of fraud and faced a Star Chamber hearing. He was succeeded by his eldest son, Theophilus Howard, 2nd Earl of Suffolk (1584–1640), on 28 May 1626. A package of positions included that of Lord-Lieutenant of Dorsetshire and the town of Poole. Lieutenant Hammon, having been a guest at Lulworth Castle, described it as 'stately.' He was particularly impressed by the tapestries, curtains and quilts of damask, silk and velvet. The lodging chambers were 'all richly hanged and adorned.' There was even a Persian carpet.

Beside Lulworth Castle was a 'fair garden and orchard walled about' which was created by Theophilus Howard in 1636. Around it stood double blocks of stables, a four-bedroom gatehouse, and a lodge. Such was the desirable real estate that became available for purchase in 1640.

The Early 1900s

Left: *The entrance steps in the middle of the eastern frontage (left) and north-east tower (centre) in a view looking south-west in 1905.*

Right: *The drawing-room, Lulworth Castle in 1926.*

Left: *The saloon, Lulworth Castle in 1926.*

Fire!

Above: *The disastrous fire at Lulworth Castle on 29 August 1929, looking westwards from an aeroplane hired by the* Daily Mail. *Rescued items from the castle were gathered in heaps on the lawns.*

Left: *A fire-ladder and the rescue operation on 29 August 1929, viewed from the west. Piles of furniture, paintings and books were saved, but the blaze was out of control in the top two floors.*

Right: *The gutted shell of Lulworth Castle. Looking north-west, the south-east tower (centre) and main entrance steps in the eastern frontage (right) can be seen.*

Restoration

Left: *Looking north-west, Lulworth Castle can be seen as a romantic ruin with ivy beginning to spread above the eastern steps. Photographed by Frederick G. Masters in 1969.*

Right: *Top-to-bottom restoration in progress above and around the back steps on the west side of Lulworth Castle in 1993. This view looks east towards the north-west tower (left).*

Left: *Opened again, by English Heritage in 1995. Showing the southern side of Lulworth Castle.*

The Castle Today

*Castle view, southwards and seawards in 1997,
over the tower of the Parish Church,
to the Arish Mell Gap.*

Right: *Entrance to the Stable Café
and Courtyard Shop, viewed from
the east in 2002.*

Left: *White Lodge Gate into
Lulworth Park, open for business,
as seen from the south in 2002.*

53

Park Lodges

Above: *Park Lodge Cottages and Lodge Wood.*

Below: *Lodge Wood with tall beeches in its south-west corner.*

Park Lodges

The North Lodges brought Georgian style to Lulworth Park.

Round tower of pretend fortifications, giving an ancient look to the park in a view towards North Lodges.

Park Lodges

This seventeenth-century East Lodge stood in front of Lulworth Castle before being moved to its present position between East Lulworth and Shaggs, where it was rebuilt in 1808.

New date – 1808 – added to the arched gateway of the 'Old Lodge'.

Chapter 7

LULWORTH & THE WELDS

The lasting name at Lulworth arrived on the scene in 1641. After the death of the 2nd Earl of Suffolk the estate was sold to Humphrey Weld of Holwell, Hertfordshire, from a Catholic family in Cheshire. He secured an even better future by marrying Clare, daughter of Lord Arundel, whose Arundel Castle was the national bastion of the 'old religion'. The Welds and money went together – grandfather Humphrey Weld, the fourth son of John Weld of Eaton by Tarporley, was Lord Mayor of London in 1608. The Lulworth Estate, however, was only partly paid for because the purchase took place during a tumultuous period in English history.

Lulworth Castle faced challenging times during the Civil War and was doubly lucky to survive. At the start of the war it was garrisoned for the Royalist cause, by Sir John Turberville of Bere Regis. By the end of the year it was held by Parliamentary foot soldiers under the command of a Captain Thomas Hughes. They melted five tons of lead, which had been stripped from the castle's roof and plumbing, and turned it into musket balls for use elsewhere in the county,

Humphry Weld (1611–85), who brought the family to Dorset, painted by Cornelius Jansen.

particularly in the siege of Corfe Castle. Battle Plain lies on the north-east edge of the Lulworth Ranges, a kilometre south of Holme Lane, westwards from Army danger flag No. 59. Its name is said to commemorate a Civil War skirmish.

A revealing document survives from 1646 that illustrates the extent of bureaucracy and Cromwellian concern to be seen to be acting above suspicion. Captain Hughes accepted personal responsibility for handing over, to the county treasurer, three puncheons

of spirit and a hogshead of wine that had been 'washed ashore from wrecks.' Few commanders in history would be so careless with the double gifts of nature and war.

Humphrey Weld bemoaned the condition of Lulworth Estate when he returned to it in 1647. Bindon House had been burnt down. In addition, the castle's water pipes, wood panelling and ironwork had been removed. The deer park palings had been destroyed. In all there had been 'great wastes and spoils committed on [his] house and lands.' To make matters worse, a guard of ten soldiers prevented anyone 'to remain or abide in the said castle that are disaffected to the Parliament.'

Renovation followed the Restoration. So did a royal visit; Charles II arrived in 1665 to escape the Great Plague which was ravaging London. He was accompanied by his brother, James Stuart, Duke of York, and James Scott, Duke of Monmouth. The latter was the King's illegitimate son. These two travelling companions contested the throne after the King's death.

In the meantime, Humphrey Weld was appointed Governor of Portland and was sent to Paris as a royal envoy. He later became the Member of Parliament for Christchurch. Everything went well for him until the alleged Popish Plot of 1679 when he was forced out of public life, and became debt-laden as he struggled to keep his art collection intact. He died in 1685. Widow Clare Weld described the castle as 'ready to drop down' when it was inherited by nephew William Weld.

He did his best to hold the line but the castle may have lost much of its furniture. The next

Humphrey Weld (died 1722) married Margaret Simeon in 1700, who brought a dowry of £5,000. Double taxation threatened Catholic fortunes at this time and Lulworth's entry in the Register of Papist Estates, in 1717, shows that it was still facing difficulties. Five years later, Edward Weld (1705–61) inherited his father's estate.

He married the Honourable Catherine Elizabeth Aston, daughter of Lord Aston, in an arranged marriage between the two Catholic families. The union soon failed, however, and in 1731 husband and wife faced each other in the Arches Court at Canterbury where Catherine filed a suit for nullity on the grounds of Edward's impotency. He had undergone treatment for what was described as 'a physical abnormality.' This medical evidence enabled him to successfully defend the case.

The secondary issue concerned Catherine's alleged libel in bringing the original action. This was also determined in Edward's favour. As a result the nation was able to enjoy the details twice over, in pamphlets on *The Cases of Impotency and Virginity Fully Discuss'd, being the Genuine Proceedings in the Arches Court*, and a *Sequel to the Case*. The latter document comprised 18 letters that had been sent between the couple, after Catherine went home to Staffordshire, where she died in 1739. This released Edward Weld to marry Mary Teresa Vaughan the following year. She redeemed his reputation with the first of five children.

A new golden age was around the corner. The insertion of the castle's classical entrance may have been a Restoration touch, by the seventeenth-century Humphrey Weld, but it is more likely to have been part of the improvements carried out by the next Edward Weld (1741–75) who sponsored the Lulworth Enclosure Act of 1768 to move the village. The revamped castle entrance has an Ionic

Original Jacobean door, re-set in the eighteenth-century basement entrance at Lulworth Castle, in 1907. The door survived the fire and is now in Lulworth Castle House.

frontispiece topped with a couple of Roman emperors on pillars either side of the door. They are flanked above by lead figures from the worlds of music and painting, with another pair of statues in niches around each corner of the eastern frontage.

Edward Weld the second returned from the Grand Tour, ten months after his father's death, in September 1762. He married Juliana Petre, daughter of the 9th Lord Petre, who came with a £10,000 dowry in 1763, but she died childless in 1772. James Paine, at the height of his fame as England's leading country-house architect, was working at Wardour Castle, Wiltshire, for the Weld's Arundel kinsfolk in 1773 when he was consulted by Edward Weld. Advice was sought for a columned hall and new central staircase. The resultant plans reveal extended balustrades and basements around the north and south walls. These designs were adapted by John Tasker during the period of Thomas Weld (1750–1810). The brother of Edward Weld junr, he carried out their father's plans to move East Lulworth village and built the park wall. The castle's Jacobean fireplaces were ripped out as a country-baroque style was superimposed. The best rooms were transformed between 1727 and 1759, influenced by rococo high fashion, with fine furnishings, plaster mouldings and marble fireplaces. Much of this work has traditionally been attributed to the Bastard brothers from Blandford. They rose to fame by rebuilding their home town after it was devastated in a fire in 1731. Although they started off working as provincial builders, and used some old pattern books, they came under the influence of Thomas Archer, who designed Chettle House, and were friends of John James. Both were at the cutting edge of the neo-classical fashion that was in vogue at this time.

Thomas Bastard re-styled the castle's dining-room in 1727 and John Bastard designed a new hall in 1738. His visualisations survive in the Dorset Record Office, showing a pedimented chimneypiece, cornice and plaster-work similar to that which they provided for Nathaniel Ireson in Coupar House, Blandford. The foundation stone for a new coach-house was laid on 25 May 1753 and it was complete by September 1755.

The Bastard family and their workers were still busy on the first floor of Lulworth Castle in 1756. Contemporary accounts record the purchase of 300 yards of crimson silk damask for curtains and bedroom hangings. The wallpaper included 200 yards of 'Saxon Green mohaireen' from Strand decorator Mr Pope. It was used in the ground-floor parlour and bedroom above in what became known, from the wallpaper, as the Green Tower. Almost down-market, in comparison, was the order in June 1756 of 425 yards of 'Harrateen' for curtains and hangings in the bedrooms for lesser members of the family. Edward Weld had little need to count the pennies and none whatsoever after 1758 when he inherited the lucrative Stonyhurst estates in Lancashire, on the death of a cousin, the Duchess of Norfolk.

The finest accommodation for guests at Lulworth was the King's Room. Its rococo ceiling in pale blue, with a delicate frieze of birds and putti, showed the talent of brothers John and Thomas Bastard and the latter's son Thomas, for plaster-work as perfect as their carpentry and joinery. They

Maria Anne Smythe (1756–1837), wife of Edward Weld, went on to marry King George IV.

were still re-decorating bedrooms until July 1759, after the windows on the second floor had been glazed in square glass. Thomas Weld now had a sumptuous home.

Fanny Burney and other later visitors chuckled at stories of a Mrs Fitzherbert at Lulworth. She was Miss Maria Anne Smythe (1756–1837), from Brambridge, Hampshire, when the younger Edward Weld took her as his second wife. That was in 1775 and Edward died the same year. Portland diarist Elizabeth Pearce described Maria as 'more beautiful and gracious than almost any living woman.' On a childhood visit to France she had been introduced to Louis XV, at dinner, and was so amused to see him pull a chicken apart with his hands that he presented her with a box of sugarplums. She continued to captivate men of all ages.

In her second marriage, 22-year-old widow Mrs Maria Anne Weld took to be her husband Thomas Fitzherbert of Swynnerton, Staffordshire. The wedding was in 1778 but she was again a widow in 1781. Mrs Fitzherbert then took up residence in Richmond and 'soon became the centre of an admiring circle of admirers.' In 1785 she met and married the Prince of Wales, later George IV, but although properly conducted the ceremony was without the consent of his father, King George III, and was therefore considered invalid under the Marriage Act of 1772. Prince George, born in 1762, was aware of his constitutional problem but hoped to carry off a fait accompli. Instead he was fated to a disastrous second marriage with Princess Caroline of Brunswick (1768–1821).

Of Mrs Fitzherbert, the so-called 'morganatic wife', Elizabeth Pearce wrote:

I've heard the turn of her wrist and ankle were such as marked her birth: a high-bred woman's walk and carriage is as noted as a thorough-bred horse's, and that her countenance was wonderful out of the common. Young, and rich, and beautiful! A wife, as all believe; though still no wife in the eyes of the world. To think the son of our good King should so shame a gracious lady!

Separation was short lived. It was no scandal to the chattering classes. Mrs Fitzherbert and the Prince held a public breakfast to re-launch their extra-marital affair shortly after his marriage to Caroline in 1795. The pair shared both pleasure and pecuniary embarrassment. Often they had to borrow from servants and retainers in order to travel between London and Brighton. For Mrs Fitzherbert, however, these years were the best of her life, though she walked out of the relationship after a supposed slight in which she was seated at Carlton House 'according to her rank' as a commoner, at a dinner given in honour of Louis XVIII. King George IV remembered her with fondness for the rest of his life, asking after her while on his deathbed as he clutched her portrait, which he wore around his neck.

Her disengagement from the Lulworth estate was fraught with ill-feeling. Edward Weld had drafted a new will to give her 'everything in his power' but delayed signing it in case she became pregnant. At any event much of his property was left in trust. The most distressing detail for Maria was that the family claimed the pearls which, she insisted, Edward had given her. They finally agreed that she could keep them for life. On her death in 1837 they were returned to Lulworth. It is only to be expected for a landed family to dispute a will but they can hardly have seriously believed that Edward had merely loaned Maria her jewellery.

After Mrs Fitzherbert had enjoyed the company of her Prince, Lulworth Castle was being prepared for visits from his father, King George III, who came to sleep behind blue canopies in the domed and gilded royal bed. As a result of the scale of his refurbishments, Thomas Weld became known to the family as 'Thomas the Builder'. He also picked up the delightful title of 'the handsomest small man in England.' His architect was John Tasker, a fellow Catholic, from Mortimer Street, Mayfair. He designed a Pompeian Crichel-style ceiling for the drawing-room. Out went John Bastard's plasterwork in the Great Hall, in 1780, to be replaced by what Jean Manco and Francis Kelly describe as 'an

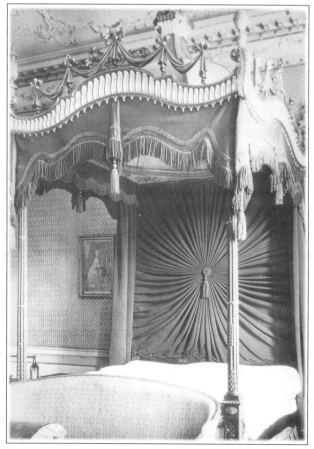

The King's Room and its royal bed was the greatest of the treasures lost in the 1929 fire at Lulworth Castle (note the picture of Princess Caroline of Brunswick). Photographed by E. Dodshon in 1926.

understated elegance that provides the perfect backdrop to the gallery of family portraits in frames made to match.' It also had good acoustics, as an organ by Seede of Bristol was encased behind a partition at the west end of the room.

John Tasker also designed the Palladian-style Great Chapel in Lulworth Park, a short distance inland from Lulworth Castle, which has a notable place in ecclesiastical history, being the first purpose-built Catholic church in England since the Reformation of 1539. The Gordon riots had taken place in 1780. Catholics had been given back partial freedom by the Relief Act of 1778. Permission for the Lulworth building was granted by George III, although the Weld family tradition is that he stipulated it should look more like a Greek temple or mausoleum than a Christian church. Work started in December 1785 with 'quarrying stone at Bindon Warren, taking down stone at Bindon Abbey' and 'Worbarrow stone for the plinth' or foundations.

Cut stone for facing the main building was brought by sea from Portland, via Lulworth Cove and Worbarrow Bay, and the altar was put in place in 1787. Bodies and monuments are said to have been brought from the Parish Church at East Lulworth to validate the pretence that the building was a mausoleum. There is no surviving record of the consecration of the church, dedicated to the Blessed Virgin Mary, which must have been regarded as a matter private to Catholics. However, the church assumed a higher profile in 1790 when it was used to consecrate the American prelate John Carroll as Bishop of Baltimore, Bishop Douglas of London, and Bishop Gibson of the North of England.

Thomas Weld also moved some of the village, from beside the castle, to a 'New Village' which is now East Lulworth. Ten acres of banks, hollows and house-platforms mark the site of the original village, south of the stables, and old maps show meadows on the north side of these buildings. Formal gardens, no longer fashionable, were destroyed in about 1750, in favour of new-style parkland grounds. The old stables, between the castle and church, were also removed. Their replacement, the present Stable Courtyard, incorporates an earlier building but was almost completely rebuilt and given a 1777 datestone. Only St Andrew's Church remained.

The clearances, over a decade, were designed to create walled parkland. Lulworth Park Wall encloses 550 acres of park and woodland, and is four miles in circumference. It is constructed of gritty brown heath-stone, architecturally known as carstone, although later repairs have brick above. It rises in places from five feet to ten feet, with embattled parapets. This design ensured the containment of a fallow deer herd. Six round towers, each six feet in diameter and 15 feet high, are set at angles in its course. Construction, which took about 20 years, was commemorated by the 1785 gate piers of the North Lodges.

Above: *The Catholic chapel amid the rhododendrons, as seen from the south-west, showing how it met George III's edict that the classical lines of the building should look more like a temple than a church.*

Right: *Inside the dome of the Catholic chapel, which is dedicated to Saint Mary, looking eastwards to the richly-adorned altar.*

East Lodge, a two-storey building with parapets above an arched carriageway, has an 1808 datestone but this merely records its rebuilding in the present position. It actually dates from the seventeenth century and originally stood in the courtyard in front of the castle. Having been taken down in 1753, it had lain in heaps for half a century, before Thomas Weld decided to have it rebuilt as his 'Wareham Lodge' entrance.

George III, the Queen, and their princesses sailed in from Weymouth in 1789. A repeat visit took place in 1791. There should have been another in 1792 but heavy seas prevented the royal family landing, with the exception of the Prince of Wales, who jumped ashore but was soaked in the process. The remainder of the party arrived by carriage a few days later. George III came back again later in the year, on his fourth visit to Lulworth Castle. He also visited West Lulworth in 1801. That was in order to see the hostelry, the Red Lion, in which dramatist John O'Keeffe had discovered his character John

Barleycorn. A contemporary print shows the royal party in Lulworth Park, including King George III (leaning on a walking stick), the Queen and the Prince of Wales, as well as Princess Caroline of Brunswick (with a Pekinese) whom he was forced to marry in 1795.

Thomas Weld repeatedly refused to join the Catholic Committee which was lobbying to remove the last legal restrictions on the faith. He reluctantly signed a 'Declaration and Protestation by the Catholics of England' having warned that it might backfire by hardening Protestant attitudes. He took part in a deputation to Prime Minister William Pitt in 1790 to register opposition to a proposed legal definition of 'Protesting Catholic Dissenters'. This was removed from the second Relief Act which received the royal assent on 10 June 1791.

Thomas Weld often disappointed his friends by arguing as a realist and pragmatist. He told them that no further major relaxation of the law in respect of Roman Catholics would be possible for at

The Welds & Lulworth Castle

*Royal visitors to Lulworth Castle, c.1800, featuring the Prince of Wales with Princess Caroline
of Brunswick (with Pekinese) and King George III (with walking stick) and the Queen,
in a view south-westwards from Lulworth Park to the sea.*

*Lulworth Cove in the eighteenth century, in the time of Thomas Weld.
Looking south, a stone-built pier is on the inner shore.*

least a generation. His friend George III had made it clear that the coronation oath prevented him from consenting to further legal relaxations.

Thomas Weld also invited refugee French Trappist monks to East Lulworth, in 1794, and provided them with Monastery Farm, which would be their home until 1817.

The next Thomas Weld (1773–1837) went further, progressing from family man to Catholic Cardinal in 1830. In 1796 he married Lucy Bridget Clifford. Their only child, Mary Lucy Weld, was born at Upwey, in Weymouth, in 1799. When his wife died at Clifton in 1815, Thomas Weld began to reconsider his life, and with Mary's marriage to her second cousin, the 7th Baron Clifford, he felt free to join the Catholic ministry.

Thomas Weld renounced the family property in favour of his next brother, Joseph Weld (1777–1863), and was ordained priest in 1821. His first postings were to Chelsea and Hammersmith followed by a rise in the ecclesiastical ranks to Bishop Coadjutor of Kingston, and his own consecration as Bishop of Lower Canada and Amycia in 1826. Rome was next, in 1830, and he heard only a few hours later than Pope Pius VIII was to honour him with the purple. Thomas Weld was the second Englishman to be admitted to the College of Cardinals since the death of Cardinal Howard in 1694. He lived in the Odescalchi Palace and died in 1837. He is buried in the church of San Marcello al Corso and was unique as a Catholic in having received all seven sacraments.

Back at Lulworth, in the English Channel, Joseph Weld became one of the foremost Victorian yachtsmen. His boats *Arrow*, *Lulworth* and *Alarm* won races at

Thomas Weld (1773–1837) progressed from landowning family man to Catholic Cardinal.

Joseph Weld (1777–1863) designed and skippered racing yachts.

Cowes and he was one of the founders of the Royal Yacht Squadron. On the estate he also had water on his mind, damming the valley north of Home Farm in 1837 to create The Lake. He built a miniature fort towards the northern end of the wild western shore, which he used as the boathouse for a brig he designed for the Admiralty. The idea was to test this and the models of racing yachts. His successful projects earned £3,000 in prize money.

Joseph Weld's son, Edward, inherited Lulworth Castle in 1863 and set about selecting an architect to sort out the problem with the stairs, which James Paine had been asked about and John Tasker had only partly solved. He chose the Catholic architect Joseph Aloysius Hansom, of Hansom cab fame, the founding editor of *The Builder*. This constituted a substantial rearrangement of the interior, during which a lift, water closets, baths and central heating brought modern amenities.

The fortune and status of the Welds took an upward turn in 1840 when Thomas Weld (1808–87), Joseph's second son and secretary to his uncle Cardinal Weld, inherited the huge Ince Blundell Estates in Lancashire and assumed the additional name Blundell. His son, Charles Joseph Weld-Blundell (1845–1927), threw himself into Darwinian natural science and travelled Latin America for three years, gathering information and observations to prove that birds of prey hunted by sight rather than smell. The results were published in *The Times* in October 1872.

As a result of this intimate knowledge of jungle terrain, Lord Clarendon sent Charles back to South America, on a special mission to advise on whether diplomatic relations should be resumed with the Bolivian Republic. For the Government of Melgarejo he mapped and studied previously unexplored country between the Vermejo and Pilcomayo rivers and the land of the Abas.

Returning to Dorset, at the age of 40 in 1884, Charles faced up to the responsibilities that went with succeeding to his father's Lancashire estates and consequently decided that his travelling days were over. He linked the Weld line with that of another powerful family, by marrying Charlotte Lane-Fox, and told family and friends that henceforth he would concentrate on art, politics and journalism. Never at a loss for a strong opinion he wrote for the *Dublin Review, Liverpool Mercury, The Tablet* and *Catholic Times*. His special subject in polemic articles were expanded into a book, *The Church of the Tithe*.

Weld-Blundell's politics quivered on the cusp between old-Tory certainties and new-Whig radicalism. Having opted for the latter but failed to win the Parliamentary seat of Preston, in 1885, Charles was promised Chatham as consolation by the Liberal caucus. His free-thinking on the Newcastle administration, and against curbing the House of Lords, caused the offer to be withdrawn, or 'tabooed' as Weld-Blundell put it.

This convinced him to leave his London residence – Blundell House on Campden Hill, Kensington – and embark on the third phase of his life. He managed and transformed the massive family estates around Liverpool. Along the shore from Southport to Formby Point, he was particularly proud of having established vast pine plantations, in a succession of winter plantings across bare sand-dunes. At home he was the curator of the biggest private collection of Greek and Roman marble sculpture in Britain. Ince Blundell Hall and Lydiate Hall were hard work but Lulworth was for summer and pleasure. Charles was the heir to the Dorset estates, which were his ancestral heritage, and re-established the link between Lulworth and the Crown by entertaining King George V in 1912, his coronation year.

Having allowed the newly-formed Tank Corps to train at Lulworth he regarded it as a bitter betrayal when the Government decided the Army should remain after the Armistice. Weld-Blundell put his views to the national newspapers with characteristic bluntness: 'Even the Hun never did anything like this!'

Herbert Weld (1852–1935), son of Thomas Weld-Blundell and brother of Charles, was a remarkable archaeologist, naturalist and explorer. His travels began in Persia in 1891 and led to an expedition to Persepolis where he obtained the moulds for relief replicas in the British Museum and the Louvre, and planned the reconstruction of the ancient city. In Africa he crossed Somalia and Abyssinia to Sudan, mapping the country, collecting and big-game hunting. He brought back 330 bird specimens, of which 17 were new species, and presented them to the Natural History Museum in 1899.

Parkland oaks in a winter view looking westwards to the eastern frontage of Lulworth Castle, in 1905, after trees closer to it had been felled.

The following year Herbert headed for South Africa as a correspondent for the *Morning Post* during the Boer War. A return to what is now Ethiopia, in 1905, resulted in the first detailed maps of the Blue Nile from Tsana down to Sudan. After the First World War he planned and self-financed his biggest archaeological adventure. Herbert Weld led a team that travelled across Iraq in 1922 and excavated ancient Kish at Tell Aheimar. Thousands of inscribed tablets and other antiquities were brought back for the Ashmolean Museum in Oxford.

On 19 September 1927 Herbert visited Thomas Hardy at Max Gate, Dorchester, and had the distinction of being the subject of the last entry that Hardy made in his personal notebook, four months before the novelist died: 'Mr Weld of Lulworth Castle, and Sir F. and Lady Keeble (Lillah McCarthy) called.'

For pleasure Herbert went yachting and the shock of the fire at Lulworth Castle on 29 August 1929 was mitigated by the fact that most of his priceless ancient finds were safe in national museums.

Charles Weld's son, Richard Weld (1887–1916), was married to Mary Mayne. After his death, she married the poet Alfred Noyes, in 1927. Mary Noyes successfully sued the Weld family in 1929 for heirlooms as a result of Richard's contested will.

The fire that year at Lulworth Castle destroyed the interior decoration and immovable items of furniture, including the historic royal bed, but precious paintings and smaller treasures were salvaged from the lower floors before the house was gutted. The Luttrell Psalter, which is now in the British Museum, had already been removed from the house.

The blaze started on the top floor and was probably caused by 'fused electric wires'. Exterior walls remained intact and have since been restored, as a romantic ruin, by English Heritage. Work started after it was taken into guardianship by the Directorate of Ancient Monuments and Historic Buildings in 1981.

The Weld family seat is now Lulworth Castle House. Colonel Sir Joseph William Weld (1909–92), Herbert's first cousin once removed, the son of Wilfrid Joseph Weld (1849–1924) of Avon Dassett,

The Family Seat

Above: *Lulworth Castle House, replacement residence of the Welds, seen across Lulworth Park from the south-east in 2002.*

Below: *The Stables and Weld estate office at Lulworth Castle, viewed from the south-east in 1907.*

Warwickshire, married Elizabeth Bellord in 1933 and inherited the Lulworth Castle estate in 1935. Unknown to him it was an even richer heritage than he realised. In 1988 Sir Joseph heard from Michael Jeffe of the Fitzwilliam Museum, Cambridge, that he was the lucky possessor of a previously unrecorded Rubens. He told the story at the foundation-laying ceremony for a hospice. The previously unattributed drawing of The Circumcision had been bought in Genoa by Richard Houlditch. On his death in 1760 it was sold to William Roscoe. At the disposal of his collection, in 1816, the buyer was Charles Robert Blundell of Ince Blundell Hall, which came to the Welds by marriage. 'It's not every day you find you own a Rubens,' claimed Sir Joseph.

Lieutenant-Colonel Joe Weld served in the Second World War, initially as adjutant of the 4th Battalion, the Dorsetshire Regiment, and then as the first Territorial Officer to be on the permanent staff in the Staff College at Camberley. From 1943 he was General Staff Officer I for Lord Louis Mountbatten in the London headquarters of South East Asia Command. Lady Edwina Mountbatten had been left in his care and was re-inventing herself, from an unconventional multi-millionairess, both socialite and socialist, into a latter-day Florence Nightingale.

After D-Day she accompanied Joe Weld and General Bertram Sergison-Brooke of the Red Cross in an American VIP B17 Flying Fortress borrowed from General Dwight D. Eisenhower, Supreme Commander Allied Forces, to Normandy to visit military field hospitals and French civilian hospitals. Both were far busier than had been expected. Edwina's appearances were recalled by FANY officers (First Aid Nursing Yeomanry) as rather inspirational, even theatrical:

Lieutenant-Colonel Joe Weld accompanied Lady Mountbatten on her tour of field hospitals during the Second World War.

Except it was not acting – it was real – her visits were like a performance by a great actress. She had long since learnt her part perfectly and knew the cues and entrances and all that. But every time it was like the first night. She put her all into every performance – and was perfection. And I suppose that's what makes a great actress. It certainly made a great head of a great nursing organisation.

Colonel Weld witnessed it from the sharp end, at her side, on a quick and continuous succession of visits in which they had authority to go anywhere. Ensuring they arrived at each destination involved a gruelling schedule:

A few quick repairs to her make-up were followed by a brisk combing of her hair, patting it neatly into place and planting her hat attractively on top. Then out came a clothes brush to flick off stray powder and loose hairs from her collar, lapels and shoulders.

They risked shelling and mines, on the roads, as well as attack from the Luftwaffe and flak when in the air. Their closest shave came in October 1944 near Nijmegen after the Dutch town was captured by the United States 82nd Airborne Division. Edwina had been loaned a twin-engined Avro Anson with a New Zealand pilot who lost his bearings and strayed over German lines. Suddenly they were a sitting target amid bursting anti-aircraft fire at 400 feet and an engine was lost as flak riddled the aircraft. One of the party was hit in the face: 'The pilot just managed to hedge-hop back over our lines, and the journey had to be completed by jeep.'

The High Sheriff of Dorset, in 1951, Colonel Weld was Lord Lieutenant for the county from 1964 to 1984, being knighted in 1973. He was chairman and then president of South Dorset Conservative Association and chaired the Wessex Regional Hospital Board during its transition into Wessex Regional Health Authority.

As chairman of the local police committee he was renowned for remembering the names of every officer he had ever met. 'Not just policemen, those of everyone he met,' I was told.

'I put a curse on you and you will die,' Colonel Weld was told by a gypsy, as he imposed a fine as chairman of Wareham magistrates. 'Thank you, madam,' he replied in his usual courteous manner. 'I'll take a chance on that.' Some 40 years later, on his death, the estate passed to his son. Wilfrid Weld (born 1934) heads the family into the new millennium.

Chapter 8

THE LAST OF THE TURBERVILLES

The lost Turberville family mansion at Bere Regis, since levelled, at Court Green.

An inscription in a small field called Canary Close, near the vicarage at East Lulworth, recorded the demise of one of the last members of the medieval Turberville family of Bere Regis and Woolbridge Manor, whose legend spurred Thomas Hardy to write *Tess of the d'Urbervilles*. The last of the line at Lulworth was John Turberville or Turbeville (in its evolution the spelling dropped the second 'r') whose gravestone hinted at a lost past:

In Memory of John Turberville, gent, who died in the ninth day of August, 1703, in assured hope by the merits of Jesus Christ to receive a better inheritance. Also for Mary his wife who died in 1716.

The southern extremity of the once-immense family estate had shrunk in his will to a small field at East Lulworth known as Canary. He also held 'the forsear of two acres of Hay Ground lying in West Holme

Meadow' and whatever limited number of farm stock the ground supported.

The inscription on a floor-slab in Bere Regis Parish Church records the Lulworth-Bere link: John Turberville (died 1733) of 'Beere' and Woolbridge married Ann Howard, daughter of Thomas Howard, Lord Bindon. The site of their mansion in Bere Regis, opposite the Royal Oak, is now Court Green pasture. Another largely illegible stone, dated 1710, must be for the occupant whose enigmatic coffin details, scratched in lead, were recorded when the family vault was last explored and sealed in Victorian times: 'In this coffin remaines all that is left of 4 sons & one daughter of Thomas Turberville [words unclear] was entered in this vault, June ye 24, 1710.' Another inscription is to 'Robert Turberville Esq. dyed May ye 6 1710 in ye 37 year of his age.' A Bere Regis historian identifies this Robert Turberville as the younger brother of Thomas Turberville, who was the last lord of the manor.

The latter succeeded their father Thomas Turberville (1621–1701) but died less than three years later, on 3 February 1704. This Thomas Turberville had four sons though they are all said to have died at an early age: 'Thomas in 1699, John and Robert in 1701, and George in 1702.' This genealogy would only begin to make sense if Robert's demise digits have been transposed, and he actually died in 1710.

The Thomas Hardy version of the story is a lot closer to fact than we might think. Fred Pitfield records that the name of this once powerful but now extinct family has persisted in a corrupt form:

In fact, in the middle of the nineteenth century there was a poor family of Torevilles living in Bere Regis, one of whom, believing himself to be the rightful heir of the Turbervilles, was said to have insisted on calling himself 'Sir John'.

There is a tradition concerning the bricked up doorway in the south aisle of the church. It is said that a Turberville, when lord of the manor, had a difference of opinion on some matter with the vicar at the time, and as a result vowed that he would never again enter the church through the existing doors. But they later became reconciled, and the lord of the manor, in order to resume his attendance at church and at the same time not break his vow, arranged for a new door opening to be made. More probably the opening was a 'mason's door', made as a temporary opening to facilitate some extensive building works.

Four decades ago, when the author was travelling around by hitchhiking and bus, there were still pre-Hardy versions of the Turberville story in general circulation. Mary E. Bradley, then living at Durweston,

gave an account of the 'spectral coach' seen travelling between Bere Regis and Woolbridge Manor that could only be seen 'by those with Turberville blood in their veins.' There was also the legend of meteor storms marking the passing of the family's last relict females.

I have tried to reconcile records of both events. The end of the female line rested with the three daughters of Thomas Turberville senr. Mary, who married Major William Ducket, died in 1749. There was also Mary Trenchard, who married younger Thomas Turberville, as the 'Widow and Co-heirs of Esqr Turberville' appear in the churchwardens' accounts for receipt of parochial dues. The first Mary's sisters, twins Elizabeth and Frances, never married. The three sisters sold the manor to Henry Drax of Charborough Park in 1833 and went to London. They lived together at Purser's Cross, Fulham, and died within days of each other, being buried together at Putney in February 1780.

In an age when lights in the sky could be regarded as portents of disastrous events, Lulworth Castle was treated to a spectacular meteor sighting at 9p.m. on the first Saturday of December in 1762. A contemporary newspaper cutting in an album in Dorset County Museum records that a 'sudden and radiant light over-spread the earth and sea, equal to the splendour of the noon-day sun.' The correspondent reports that:

... looking directly over us we saw an appearance reful-gent [dazzling] as the Sun itself, in form straight at a line, about eight times the diameter of the full moon in length, the duration of a minute. Afterwards it altered its position and changed into a serpentine form, and seemed to terminate in smoke.

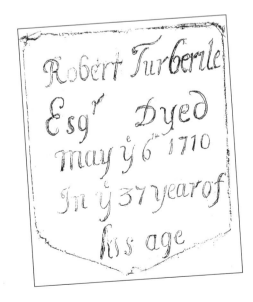 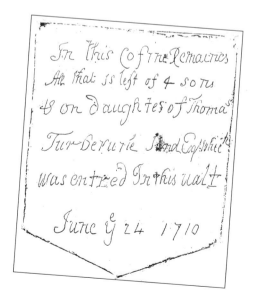

Coffin inscriptions, dated 1710, were the most recent to be found by a Victorian visitor who entered the Turberville vault in Bere Regis Parish Church.

Chapter 9

'TALE OF A MODERN GENIUS'

Looking up the drive, from the north-west to the vicarage at East Lulworth, in 1905, when it was the home of Revd W.D. Filliter. He researched self-proclaimed 'genius' John Fitzgerald Pennie who was born there.

East Lulworth produced a noted writer. John Fitzgerald Pennie (1782–1848) was born at the vicarage where his parents were in domestic service. As with the last of the Turbervilles they could look back to better ancestry, before falling on evil days, with the Pennie tradition of a 'gold seal engraved with the family arms.' In the seventeenth century they were among the good and the great who 'bequeathed many gifts to the royal borough of Corfe Castle.'

W.D. Filliter, the Edwardian vicar of East Lulworth, found out what he could of Pennie's childhood. He was born in the vicarage on 25 March 1782. Filliter claims the vicar, Mr Milbourne, had let the property to Pennie's father. His mother was 47 years old at the time 'which circumstance, together with their narrow means, partly accounts for the strange manner of his upbringing.' Formal schooling, in his life, amounted to only seven weeks. 'My father

dislikes books,' he wrote, and 'is an enemy to everything of a literary nature so that I have to write under the garden hedge, or behind the stables and barn.' His mother instilled Pennie with an 'unnatural dislike' of normal games and play.

She, however, did encourage his love of books and his thirst for knowledge. He often slept with a copy of *Pilgrim's Progress* under his pillow and it seems that his favourite reading comprised *The Grave* and *Meditations Among the Tombs*. Much of his time was spent 'dreamily wandering over the wide heaths or through the woods around his home, or climbing the steep sides of the silent hills between us and the Channel.' As such, Filliter describes the Bindon Hill of Pennie's adventures from the departure of prehistoric warriors through to the arrival of the first tanks:

There he would lie for hours, gazing out over the sea at the ships that passed away to distant lands leaving him, as he imagined, like a bird beating its wings against the bars of a narrow cage.

Given that Pennie received little or no formal education his emergence as a child prodigy was against all the odds. Self-taught, by the age of 15 this shepherd boy had turned a tale from Robert Greene's *History of Dorastus and Fawnia* into his own tragedy, entitled *The Unhappy Shepherdess*. Having trawled through the same material that Shakespeare turned into *A Winter's Tale* he 'criticises the immortal Bard's historical and geographical inaccuracies.' Filliter expresses disappointment that John Fitzgerald Pennie had no sense of fun, and was incapable of bringing poignancy to his tragedy by lightening it with contrasting moments of humour, and failed to grasp the inherent interest of village values. 'Content to be the poet and chronicler of his own county he might have given us much that would have lived,' Filliter thinks. He suggests better subject matter would have been 'interesting pictures of village life, harvest homes, may-poles, merrymaking, smuggling stories, local legends, humours of election time.' Instead, Pennie's 'constant struggle' was to prove himself as the next Milton, Shakespeare or Byron, preferably all of these rolled into one.

While watching his flock on the downs, Pennie became intrigued with the ancient banks of Flower's Barrow hill-fort, and its Rings Hill slopes. He found bones protruding from the chalk, probably due to erosion towards the cliff, and proceeded to unearth the skeleton of a prehistoric or Romano-British resident. His description is of a huge figure, between seven and eight feet in height, but this was something of an exaggeration caused by the fact that bones tend to separate at the joints after burial. The apprentice shepherd could well have become a Victorian antiquary if he had not been otherwise distracted.

Captain Hay Forbes, a coastguard officer at Lulworth Cove, realised Pennie's potential and arranged for him to go to London. Pennie called Forbes 'a patron raised up in this barbarian spot' and claimed that he intended to reward him with 'a handsome profit' and to 'buy books with the rest.' He was found a job and a theatrical introduction.

It seems that Pennie quickly turned into a wretched ingrate. Instead of taking advantage of the opportunity he complained of this 'dirty shop in Seven Dials' and his visit to Covent Garden was another disappointment. The manager told him his work had merit but was not in a form fit for the stage. The message was to go home and write another tragedy.

He then faced the dilemma of how to provide for himself at the same time as trying to become a dramatist. Work in Bristol, as a solicitor's clerk, provided the opportunity for 'soliloquies over Chatterton in St Mary Redcliffe Church, comparing their respective lots.' The stage offered a 'sure road

The vicarage, now Glebe House, seen from the north in 2002.

Inspirational Flower's Barrow

*Coastal erosion at Flower's Barrow, where John Fitzgerald Pennie unearthed an ancient skeleton,
looking westwards to Cockpit Head and Bindon Hill*

to splendour and renown.' This uncharacteristic burst of positive thinking was followed by more reality, with a failed attempt at becoming a civil servant as a writing-clerk at the Admiralty.

This was followed by a spell as usher at a school in Honiton but again 'people [were] against him' and it left little time for the stage. He joined a troupe of travelling actors and then went off to Malta as the companion to a young officer. On arriving back in Plymouth he walked to Lulworth. Returning to London, in 1810, he married an orphan, Cordelia Whitfield. We are told they met when she saved his life as he was drowning in Weymouth Harbour. At moments like this one laments Pennie's failure to quarry his own life for Hardyesque tragedy instead of harking back to classical sources.

He became manager of the theatre in Shaftesbury but his dramatic partner, 'a young man of dashing appearance,' was the next problem, and he lost a lot of money. His own work, *Gonzanga*, was performed in Chepstow in 1814 and his tragedy *Ethelwold*, or the *Danish Pirates*, had its stage debut in Weymouth, in 1826, and progressed to the Coburg Theatre in London.

His first epic, *The Royal Minstrel*, was published in 1817. Two other works were considered by the Haymarket and Covent Garden but neither were performed.

Pennie returned to his Purbeck roots, and started a school at Lulworth, but it had closed by 1828 when he moved to Keysworth Cottage, on the Sandford side of Wareham. Friends then built him 'a modest heathland abode' at Stoborough. He named this Rogvald, for his epic published in 1823, and became a correspondent for the *Dorset County Chronicle* and *West of England Magazine*.

Under the pseudonym Sylvaticus Pennie published *The Tale of a Modern Genius, or the Miseries of Parnassus*, in 1827. It is the autobiography of an

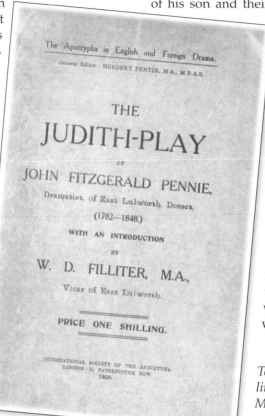

Lulworth's vicar reprinted one of Pennie's plays in 1908.

aesthete, struggling to fulfil his talent in the face of those Hardyesque obstacles. He writes it as a series of letters which are mostly addressed to 'Frank' and signed 'Sylvaticus'. The self-pity is unremitting. 'Happy villagers, your ignorance spares you the heart-rending miseries that Genius is doomed to bear,' he says, before going on to give a catalogue of those trials and tribulations of 'disappointment and sorrows.'

Life was a succession of distractions, broken promises, and debts, punctuated by hunger, sickness and lack of fuel. His final borrowings were on behalf of his son and their eventual settlement was the last achievement of his life.

Cordelia Pennie died at Rogvald (which became corrupted to Rodwell) on 11 July 1848. John was also suffering 'a painful illness' and joined her two days later. They were buried together at East Lulworth on 17 July 1848.

Their memory lived on in the village into the next century. Filliter was told that John Fitzgerald Pennie was an 'upright and honourable man' who 'wore a wig' and looked to a child 'much got up.' He was 'a bit of a poet' who 'could not write his poetry without a peacock's feather.'

The vicar concluded in 1908:

To fix Pennie's exact place in literature is not an easy task. Much that he wrote has true poetic feeling and descriptive power, but it lacks that compelling force which makes things live. A better training and a wider knowledge of the world might have induced a truer economy of words, and more severe literary restraint. Like an untrained painter, in his desire for truth, he crowds his canvas with such a mass of detail that the eye seeks in vain for rest, and the sense of proportion is lost. His works are well-nigh forgotten, even in his native county, yet it is hoped that this slight sketch may awaken some little interest in a son of Dorset who 'passed through deep waters' in his vain pursuit of lasting fame.

Chapter 10

FINDING JOHN BARLEYCORN

Irish playwright John O'Keeffe (1747–1833) visited West Lulworth in 1791 and stayed at the Red Lion in West Street which is now Churchfield House. It is beside the corner with the Main Road, and Paul Randall, who regards it as his ancestral home, tells me that it is has also served as a turnpike toll-gate. The innkeeper at the time of O'Keeffe's visit was William Randall (1728–94) who the dramatist immortalised on the London stage as his bucolic character John Barleycorn. Randall lived with wife Ann and they had five daughters and one son.

William Randall inspired O'Keeffe to produce *The London Hermit* or *Rambles in Dorsetshire*, which opened on 29 June 1793. A comedy in three acts, it was 'performed with universal applause at the Theatre Royal, Haymarket', to quote its first edition title-page of 1793. The book is dedicated to Revd John Ball of Winfrith Newburgh in gratitude for his 'hospitable roof' and 'the comforts I there enjoyed in the little parlour of a country parsonage.'

O'Keeffe remembered William Randall in his *Recollections* of 1826. He was one of the great real-life discoveries who provided ideas and material for 68 of his own productions and many collaborations with other dramatists.

Kitty Barleycorn, the publican's daughter in the comedy, is also depicted as showing aspirations beyond her station in life. John Grum, appearing as 'Jahn', is a country bumpkin whose entire vocabulary consists of 'Hum'. There is also a young prankster, defined as 'the greatest rogue in England.' The best image is what can be done 'with a bit of chalk and charcoal making a whole room of family portraits squint down upon everybody.' The text also included references to current events. John Barleycorn says that 'Parson Jack be making collections for the poor sufferers that was burnt out there at Minehead' which brings forth a debate about the merits of providing for 'the poor of another county.'

King George III arriving at the Red Lion Inn in West Lulworth to pay homage to the hostelry that provided dramatist John O'Keeffe with the inspiration for his character John Barleycorn on the London stage.

The King himself, George III, came by coach from Weymouth to visit the Red Lion in 1802. John Barleycorn died in 1794, only a year after achieving legendary status, and the royal party was received by his son, Matthew Randall. Henry Corbould painted the scene, exhibiting the canvas at the Royal Academy in 1807, and embarked on commissions from the British Museum that lasted for three decades, drawing Lord Elgin's marbles and other classical sculptures.

In his memoirs, O'Keeffe quotes the local wisdom that the sea represents discomfort and the danger of drowning, rather than being a source of pleasure. He was told by a boatman:

I keep out of the water as much as I can, and I am sure I cannot see why, for my part, you London folks come down here at vast expense to souse and sop yourself in salt water.

O'KEEFFE THRIVED ON GOSSIP WHICH HE REGARDED AS THE CEMENT OF ENGLISH CULTURE. HE TREATED RANDALL TO A KINDLY VIGNETTE:

The greatest original in person, manner and dress ever seen. He was tall, thin and bony, with a long shallow face and staring eyes. His dress usually a white flannel coat, scarlet waistcoat with brass buttons, brown corduroy breeches, brown thread stockings and thick solid shoes with iron buckles. Besides performing the duties of innkeeper to perfection he was a man of all trades. He farmed the land, mended the doors and windows, and repaired roofs. He painted names on the sterns of the local fishing boats charging a penny a letter. He was adept at cobbling shoes and had painted the Red Lion on his own sign-board. To amuse himself he strummed a bass viol and Sundays sang in the church choir. If need arose, he was always ready to act as a courier carrying messages to Poole, Blandford or Dorchester. When speaking, he gesticulated wildly, swinging his arms and head about, and continually stammering over the many long and fine sounding words with which he attempted to embellish his speech.

The Red Lion, now Churchfield House in West Road, West Lulworth, seen from the south-west in 2002.

Chapter 11

NAPOLEON & LULWORTH COVE

A short story, *A Tradition of 1804*, written by Thomas Hardy in 1882, arose from the belief that Napoleon had landed secretly at Lulworth Cove in an attempt to discover whether it was a favourable starting point to use during an invasion of England. One can hardly think of a less suitable one. In Hardy's version of the story, shepherd Job Selby and his nephew Solomon are tending their flock on Bindon Hill as two men arrive in a small boat. The nose and profile of 'Corsican ogre' and French Emperor Napoleon Bonaparte (1769–1821) cause them consternation.

The local legend, as recorded by a member of the Women's Institute during the 1930s, is that Napoleon was seen by a young farmer's wife who spoke French and heard him mutter 'impossible' as he folded his charts and walked back towards his ship. He was wearing his famous cocked hat, which was by no means unique to the Emperor, although on the other hand his features were well known from caricatures and cartoons. The story is delivered with detail of the sort rarely found in folklore:

Emperor Napoleon demonised in caricature as the Corsican ogre, spinning his way across the map of Europe, at a time when he is said to have stepped ashore in Lulworth Cove.

The incident was watched and the conversation overheard by a local farmer's wife who had learnt French as a girl so that she might help her father, a china merchant, in his business. This lady was born in 1784, and lived to be 104, and was alive when the West Lulworth contributor first heard the story.

The most likely year for this visit was 1805, after Napoleon became Emperor, and was personally supervising an invasion fleet being assembled at embarkation points along eastern parts of the Channel coast. For 80 days he was based at Pont-de-Briques, a château near Boulogne, and the period is intensely documented. There are, however, a few days in which Napoleon's movements are unknown.

In theory, he could have slipped across to England but the fact is that despite a succession of security concerns in Dorset it was Caesar's Coast – as the War Office of the 1940s later came to call the coastline of Sussex and Kent – that remained the key objective of the Grande Armee. This strategic decision would have been made based on the tides, as David Cooper convinced me in 1969. He revealed that despite the fact that 'the ebb out of Boulogne would take the fleet to the west, the flood tide along the English coast would bring it back eastwards.' It would also be pushed up-Channel by prevailing south-westerly winds.

There was no prospect of the French invading Lulworth from Boulogne. Nearer and easier were the great sandy beaches around Poole Bay – although the Grande Armee was in no position to visit them either. Nor was French intelligence so lacking that it needed to ascertain

GENERAL ORDERS,

to Lieutenants of Divisions, Superintendants of Towns and Hundreds, and Commandants of Cavalry and Infantry Volunteers, &c. &c. &c.

As a considerable agitation in Men's Minds would naturally take place, upon any appearance of an Enemy off the Coast, the different Duties required of every Individual cannot be too often repeated, and inculcated, as the surest means of preventing hurry and confusion upon such an Event, I will begin therefore with the first possible means by which the appearance of an Enemy may be notified; viz. The sudden lighting of any one Beacon; and I will here observe, that I take it for granted, the guard placed over the different Beacons, is possitively instructed, not to light his Beacon without consulting the Gentleman under whose particular direction the Beacon was set up or erected, or at least his Bailiff, or some intelligent Person, appointed to be consulted by that guard, in case of such an appearance. So far for one Beacon, and now I will suppose all the Beacons to have been fired, by proper Directions; in that case the Lieutenants of Divisions—the Superintendants, &c. of Hundreds—the Commandants of Volunteers both Cavalry and Infantry, and in short every Person holding a Command, of any Description, great or small, is to look upon the firing these Beacons, as a *Caution* and *Signal for* PREPARATION *to act*, but on no account to put any body in motion, until a particular Order is received from the Commander in Chief—from the Generals of the District—or from the Lord Lieutenant. It will be understood by this, that the assembling of the Cavalry and Infantry Volunteers, at their different Places of Rendezvous and private Parades; that the collecting the Stock, particularly of riding and draft Horses; the assembling of all Corps, viz Pioneers, Guides, and Pikemen, might take place in the different Parishes, upon the lighting of the Beacons; but that no Person without Authority, or without receiving Orders, will presume to move from the Parish. The advantages arising from this state of Preparation are obvious, and it is good to observe here, that many Hours must of necessity intervene, between the lighting of the Beacons, and the near approach of the Enemy to the Coast; no hurry therefore need take place, even in the inferior Persons, such as Drivers of Waggons, of Cattle and of Sheep; and for the same Reason no impatience need arise in Men's Minds, upon not receiving immediate Orders to put themselves in motion; but they may rely with confidence upon receiving those Orders, at the different Parishes, in full Time for their due Execution; the Cavalry and Infantry Volunteers may likewise depend upon receiving their Orders at their different Places of Rendezvous and Private Parades. The necessity of waiting for Orders, in the different Parishes must be obvious, in as much as it is the only means of avoiding Confusion; but I will take this opportunity, of strongly impressing upon every Individual that the issuing Orders for the Removal of the Stock of one Parish or Place, does not of course imply the necessity of moving the Stock of another. DATED at MILTON ABBEY, the 20th Day of March, 1804.

Signed by Order of the Lord Lieutenant,

Edwd Boswell

Clerk of the General Meetings.

DIVISIONS.	BEACONS.	Under whose direction the Beacons have been erected
Wareham		
Wimborne	Woodbury Hill	R. E. D. Grosvenor. Esq.
	Lytchet	Wm. Trenchard, Esq.
Blandford	Badbury	Henry Bankes, Esq.
	Milton Abbey	Earl of Dorchester
Shaftesbury	Woolland	Ditto
Dorchester	Melbury	Mr. Edward Buckland
	Piddletown Heath	—— George Boswell
Beaminster	Blagdon	Hon Lionel Damer
	Shipton Gorge	Mr. Richard Roberts
	Norchard Hill	—— Bernard Cox
	Pilsdon	—— Giles Symonds

'General Orders' in the event of French invasion, issued by the Earl of Dorchester at Milton Abbey and signed by county clerk Edward Boswell, in 1804.

landing conditions on the Dorset coast. Information about England and its defences had been collected for centuries. Napoleon, as David Cooper explained, approved 'the sending of spies to England and of corsairs to capture English peasants and fishermen for interrogation.'

Despite that it would have been in character for Napoleon to have taken a day off for the express purpose of enjoying a few steps on English soil. It would have been much less risky to have done that in a poorly defended corner of Dorset rather than along the actual coast that was the target for 2,000 landing craft carrying 100,000 men. There might well have been plans for diversionary moves to draw the English fleet down-Channel towards Dorset and Devon.

Napoleon kept up the pressure from Brest for this express purpose. It had an effect, as George III showed in June 1804 when he told the Duke of York:

I cannot deny that I am rather hurt there is any objection made to forming so large an Army of Reserves in Dorsetshire where, or in Cornwall, I think an attack more likely than in Essex, Kent or Sussex.

When the King later approved England's anti-invasion precautions he did so with the proviso that more troops should be provided in Dorset; it was believed that 'Dorset [was] one of the most vulnerable parts of the kingdom.'

Had Napoleon visited Lulworth, as the legend has it, it becomes entirely explicable that he made an about face and headed instead for Bavaria and Austria. Interestingly, Hitler did a very similar thing in his turn, consolidating failure in the Battle of Britain with an invasion of Russia.

Chapter 12

TRAPPISTS AT LULWORTH

East of abandoned Sea Vale Farm in the Arish Mell valley, immediately below the western end of the Purbeck Hills, is another derelict farmhouse. This one has a remarkable history. The ruined Abbey of Our Lady and Saint Susan, otherwise known as Monastery Farm, was the first Cistercian monastery to be established in the British Empire since the Reformation. It was the creation of a group of monks led by Pere Jean-Baptiste who left La Trappe after the suppression of the French religious houses by the National Assembly in 1790. Thomas Weld, as the head of one of Britain's oldest Catholic families, came forward to offer them safe refuge on his lands at Lulworth.

The move began in 1794 and was completed in March 1796. The monks gave thanks for their asylum and as a gesture of their gratitude undertook that in future they would drink only water. Locally, however, their presence on the Dorset coast gave rise to vilification, prejudice and rumour. Not only were they said to harbour spies but in 1803 it was reported that Jerome Bonaparte (1784–1860) was hidden at the Abbey. Napoleon's youngest brother, serving as a lieutenant on an expedition to Haiti, he had taken refuge from the British in the United States and was assumed to be attempting to slip back into Europe.

Matters were not helped by a Trappist defector who rediscovered his voice for salacious tales regarding his secret and sheltered existence. Dom Antony, the Superior, was summoned to London by the Prime Minister, Henry Addington, 1st Viscount Sidmouth, to answer the accusations. An enquiry took place which found the charges to be without

Monastery Farm, with Flower's Barrow behind, in a view towards Arish Mell (far right) drawn in 1815 when it was the Monastery of La Trappe.

foundation and was followed by tributes to the Abbot's honour and integrity. The harm was done, however, and an order was made that no subject of the British Crown could be admitted as a noviciate of the order.

Thomas Weld (1756–1810) became the target of pamphleteers. The notable publication, in 1801, was *The Canonisation of Thomas Weld*, which we know he read because an entry appears in his ledger: 'To my Canonisation, 2s.6d.' It parodied versifier Thomas Sternhold (died 1549) and his collaborator John Hopkins (died 1570) as 'Poets Laureate to the Monastery' by lampooning their metrical versions of the psalms that used to be part of the Prayer Book. Annotations were attributed to the Prime Minister, and philosopher David Hume, as well as the late great jurist Sir William Blackstone.

As the émigré monks became embroiled with invasion and spy scares, Thomas Weld issued a public notice offering a reward for tracking down the source of the stories:

Having been industriously circulated in the neighbourhood of Lulworth Castle, in the County of Dorset, that Jerome Bonaparte was concealed in the said Castle, or in a house near that place, belonging to Thomas Weld Esq., which is inhabited by some emigrant monks of the order of La Trappe, and that arms and ammunition were deposited there, which report, however difficult and impossible to be credited by well-informed persons, has nevertheless gained belief among many of the illiterate common people, we, the undersigned Magistrates of the County of Dorset, anxious to quiet the minds of such persons as may have given credit to the above report, and to satisfy them that it is unfounded as it is wicked and foolish, have examined every part of the Castle and house above mentioned, and, as might be expected, have not found any Arms and Ammunition concealed there, or any person whose appearance could give rise to the story, and we take this opportunity of cautioning all such persons against being in future misled by any reports of a similar nature, which can only be propagated by ill-disposed designing persons, to gratify their own private malice by creating unjust suspicions against a truly worthy and respectable character, who is well-known to the whole County of Dorset for his loyalty and attachment to his King and country. We were accompanied on our search by the Constable, Churchwarden, and Overseer of the Poor of the Parish of East Lulworth.

The leaflet was issued at Lulworth Castle on 14 August 1803. Its greater offence, signed by magistrates Lionel Damer and James Frampton, is that it enshrines a 226-word sentence. One wonders how they coped with translation into French! The constable was John Woodman, the churchwarden was Robert Seymour, and George Dagworthy signed as the overseer. Thomas Weld offered a reward of £100 'to be paid by Mr Mansfield, Attorney-at-Law, Dorchester, to the person or persons discovering the propagator of the above Report, on his or her conviction.'

Trappist rigours at Monastery Farm are documented in *A Pilgrimage to the Monastery of La Trappe* which is one of the rarest of Dorset books. It was published anonymously, being printed by Henry Skelton at West Street, Havant, for 'private circulation' in 1815. This tells us that after fleeing from France the Trappists had been given sanctuary in Russia. They refused to occupy the allotted lands, however, when they heard that the property had been seized by the State on their behalf, from peasant farmers. The Tsar was infuriated at the rejection of his generosity and deported the monks to Hamburg.

Thomas Weld offered them the coastal valley inland from Arish Mell, beneath Flower's Barrow hillfort, and erected a monastery of 'quadrangular shape, with schilling on the inside, forming the cloisters; and in the area a depository for the dead.' Here the unknown visitors from Havant saw seven graves, in the spring of 1813, some of which had 'a wooden cross', 'either at the head or feet.' They came away with the impression that the living resided with their dead, being 'continually reminded of their mortal state' as there was always an open grave, 'for the reception of the next that dies.' Burial was undertaken without any ceremony, coffin or rites and then the next grave was dug. 'Each individual prayed sincerely that he himself might soon become the occupier.'

Someone inserted critical extracts from 'a private letter' into a copy of the book:

The Superior, the Law Agent, and the Porter were alone dispensed from the extreme vigour of the vow of silence. The other members of the community were allowed one last word to their fellow creatures, but that in the agony of death, and to confess their past transgressions. A wretch extended on an iron couch

Summertime frontage, viewed from the west, of Monastery Farm in about 1900.

excited all his commiseration, for though he was writhing with pain, he was not deemed sufficiently ill to be allowed to explain the symptoms of his malady to the medical brother who consequently prescribed as it is natural to presume with unaided conjectural science. In a word, everything in and connected with the establishment seemed revolting to the mind of a civilised being, the substitution of devotional practices to the true maxims of our holy religion.

Visitors were received at the porter's lodge on the west side of Monastery Farm. The porter wore a long brown robe of coarse cloth and a cowl over his head. Keys dangled from a leather girdle around his waist. He did speak, in a whisper, but only to tell everyone to be silent. Nothing beyond eyes and noses were visible as the other monks glided along, concentrating on meditation.

Their chapel was neat and elegant but lacking decoration. There was a turret and dome rising from the centre. The high altar had a crucifix. Under a tabernacle there were terracotta or wooden relief panels featuring the Virgin and Child. Each monk had his own named stall. In all there had been 86 of them at East Lulworth. The cells where they slept had wooden beds with a single blanket and a coarse rug. Compartments were grouped together 'like so many caves of death.' The monks, or what little of them could be seen, looked well. They were fed from the surrounding land 'with the assistance of a carter and his boy' and produce surplus to their restricted diet was sent for sale to Poole.

Waking time was at 1a.m. throughout the year and devotions in the chapel followed for eight hours. Manual labour, with prayer breaks, continued into the afternoon. Their one meal of the day took place at 1.30p.m. and consisted entirely of vegetables. Reading, meditation and prayers took up the rest of the waking day. They went to bed at 8p.m.

Drinking nothing but water served to emphasise the extent of worldly deprivation. These ascetics had little else to give up having left France with the vow that if they could find permanent asylum somewhere in Europe they would show their thanks by giving up all other drinks. Their reward was in another world, beyond Heaven's gate, 'far from the world's deceiving path we fly. To find a passage to Eternity.'

As the anonymous author observed, having catalogued self-constraints and denials, the people of Dorset had 'no fear that the silent order of La Trappe [would] ever extend its influence into the neighbouring villages.' The community was raised to the status of an Abbey in 1813. Its first Abbot, Dom Antony, was a Sorbonne literateur and doctor, in earlier life Charles Saulnier de Beauregarde. He had to face the reality that with the ban on British recruitment, though a handful of children and novices had been forthcoming, there was no long-term future for Trappists at Lulworth.

Trappist Deaths at Lulworth

Between 1796 and 1816, listed in chronological order, the following 25 members of the Order of La Trappe died at Lulworth. Their country of origin was France unless otherwise stated. They were buried in a walled enclosure, 36 feet by 40 feet, with a Celtic cross set in the middle of the eastern wall, where the sun came up over Whiteway Hill.

*Augustine Auvrey
Pachonius le Coq
Raphael Emmerson (England, child)
Bernard Deagorreau
Augustine Michot
Basil de Gaudrion de la Guimardiere
Stephen Fluemser
Arsenius Durand
Marie Bernard
Mark Vannet
James White (England, child)
Maurice Adam
John of the Cross Pinatell
Dorotheus Baissin
Spiridion des Camps
Ignatius Kelly
Pachomius Roussel
Joachim Millea (Ireland)
Jerome Teeling (Ireland)
Muce Bernard
Columban Broock (England)
Placidus Fleming (Ireland)
James Tulk (England)
Stanislaus Besset de la Bessiere
Arsenius Power (Ireland)*

Dom Antony returned to France and purchased the Cistercian monastery of Melleray in Brittany. This was one of only two in the whole of the land that were still intact. A French frigate, *Revanche*, was sent to collect the Trappist community in July 1817. Their dead remained at Lulworth for another century and a half before being removed by Bournemouth undertaker Deric Scott for re-burial at Mount St Bernard's Abbey, Leicester. These exhumations were funded by the War Department, in 1952, when wartime-requisitioned Monastery Farm was permanently incorporated into the Lulworth Ranges. There was a strong superstitious belief around Lulworth that the dead should not be disturbed. Estate labourers involved were told they were cursed to 'an early and unnatural death.' Scott promised free burials if this should happen.

The monastic expression for moving from one establishment to another is 'change of stability.' The bodies had originally been buried in their habits, not in coffins, in unmarked graves. Bones were collected

Monastery Farm, in post-war dereliction.
Photographed from the south-west by Colin Graham in 1981.

in two batches. Having been moved first to the Lulworth Castle Chapel, then the Cistercian convent at Staplehill, Wimborne, the remains were taken by road to Leicester. Now collected into two coffins, they received a solemn Requiem Mass, sung at each stop. Their final resting place, with one on each side, is beside the grave of Dom Bernard Palmer, the first Abbot of Mount St Bernard. He had been both a novice and a priest at Lulworth.

Monastery Farm is visible from the northern rampart of Flower's Barrow hill-fort, the closest public access, when the coastal path is open during weekends and holidays. Its last farmers, evicted by the Army in 1941, were Frederick and Florence Childs who had arrived from East Chaldon in September 1934. Their son, Walter Childs, had been born three weeks before the move, and now lives in Alamein Road, Bovington. 'I am the last person still alive to have lived at Monastery Farm,' he told me with pride.

A remarkable aside to the story of La Trappe at Lulworth concerns young Irish monk James Power, known as Brother Thomas, who met and fell in love with Julia Woodforde from Galhampton, Somerset. The daughter of Militia Colonel William Woodforde, she had been staying at Cove Cottage, Lulworth, and walked the coast path. Power renounced his faith, and denounced the Trappists, being 'the Tom Monk who told all the treason.' Zealots and floggers, he said, had boiled the head of a dead baby to turn it into a 'noddle' masquerading as the relic of a saint.

Colonel Woodforde did his best to keep the renegade monk away from his daughter and Zachary Macaulay persuaded him to sail for Sierra Leone. The climate having wrecked his health, James Power tried to return, but died at sea eight days after he left the River Gambia on his way to England on 17 September 1819. Julia, who never married, died in 1873.

Chapter 13

THE KING FROM FRANCE

*Four decades after the storming of the Bastille, the exile of
the last French monarch from Paris to Lulworth in 1830
completed the revolution with Louis Phillipe
being proclaimed 'citizen King'.*

While continental Europe was in the throes of revolutionary turmoil in 1830 (resulting in the deposition of Charles X of France, to be replaced by Louis Phillipe) the English ruling class feared that they would be next. In the event, apart from some agricultural unrest, all that came across the Channel was an aged and ejected French monarch. The absolutist Bourbon leader had become increasingly unpopular after dissolving the Chamber of Deputies and censoring the press. On 2 August 1830 he abdicated. Having packed his treasures and assembled his entourage he departed from Cherbourg.

The 73-year-old exile, Charles X (1757–1836), arrived in Poole Harbour aboard the English steamboat *Comet* and disembarked at the Ballast Quay, Hamworthy, on 23 August 1830. The reception was muted but polite, with hats raised out of polite respect for his age, rather than his recent role. The Duke of Wellington, the Prime Minister, ordered the Custom

House authorities at Poole Quay not to inspect any of the King's baggage. Ten days later, £500,000 was invested in consols, and this was estimated as only a small fraction of the royal wealth, a fortune having been looted. Thus a coffer of the French state was emptied into Government stock in London.

Charles was attended by 120 courtiers and servants. The whole court headed for Lulworth Castle where the Catholic Weld family offered a sympathetic refuge. 'Voila la Bastille!' the King said on arrival. Extra rooms were found at Hethfelton House, four miles north on the estate lands beyond the River Frome, where the Holy Stream skirts a wild hillside near East Stoke. The ex-King comforted himself at Lulworth with a gentleman's pleasures, shot game on the estate preserves, and attended Mass in the chapel in the castle grounds. Every day it was noticed that he stood for some time and looked out to sea. It was not just any sea but that with the Cherbourg peninsula over the horizon and just 70 miles distant.

Wellington's Government agonised over the royal exile on the South Coast. That proximity to France was seen as a provocation which might lead to reprisals. In particular the Admiralty feared a landing to carry off the young Comte de Chambord, Duc de Bordeaux (1820–83). He was now the next in line to the French throne, chosen by Charles X as his heir and successor, when he abdicated. Diplomatic considerations, as well as the safety of the Bourbon claimant, caused Whitehall to arrange for the entire party to be moved to Holyrood at Edinburgh, although later the King went on to Prague. The Admiralty steam packet *Lightning* was sent to collect them and arrived at Poole on 14 October 1830. Six days later the King headed for 'long dark days' in Scotland. He was not unaccustomed to exile, having lived in England during the Napoleonic Wars, but then he had the hope of an eventual return across the water.

On his leaving Lulworth Castle there was a gathering in the hall and 'the English servants knelt to take leave of him.' Charles was brief and to the point: 'Goodbye, God bless you.' Villagers thronged around his carriage. The contemporary newspapers tell of their sorrow but cynics claimed this was born out of their concern that the King's departure would lead to a fall in commodity prices. Butter, eggs and poultry had been at a premium, 'for whilst the court was at Lulworth, the farmers' wives of the Isle of Purbeck got double, and sometimes treble, prices.'

Chapter 14

TALE OF THREE POETS

Above: *John Keats,
painted by Joseph Severn.*

Left: *Thomas Hardy, and
second wife Florence
Dugdale, contemplative
at the seaside in 1909.*

Thomas Hardy's poem, 'At Lulworth Cove a Century Back,' recorded John Keats's last moments on English soil and the writing at sea off Lulworth of his final sonnet. Desperately ill with consumption, the poet was told that his only hope of relief would be a warmer climate, and left London for Rome on the *Maria Crowther*, on 17 September 1820. He was accompanied by his friend and carer Joseph Severn. Progress down the English Channel became almost static.

On 28 September, languishing in prolonged calmness, the captain told the passengers they could go ashore for a short break. Severn recorded that Keats found he was in a part of Dorset 'that he already knew, and showed me the splendid caverns and grottoes with a poet's pride, as though they had been his birthright.'

They landed in Lulworth Cove and walked along the cliffs to Stair Hole and Durdle Door. Thomas Hardy (1840–1928) liked to think they travelled

further into Dorset but Keats was in no state to go visiting and the captain had restricted them to a few hours of daylight.

Hardy's links with Lulworth resumed with professional visits, to West Lulworth village, after the young novelist rejoined John Hicks in Dorchester for a second spell as an architectural assistant. That was in July 1867 and the plans for the restoration of the Parish Church are dated 30 August and 18 September 1867. Hardy made a pen-and-ink drawing of the cove in 1868. John Hicks died on 12 February 1869. Both the Lulworth project and Hardy the architect were taken on by George Crickmay of Weymouth. Lady Selina Bond laid the foundation stone that spring. Lulworth Cove appears as Lulwind Cove in *Desperate Remedies*, his first published novel, which he began writing in 1869. He has his characters Owen Graye and sister Cytherea going on a paddle-steamer trip and walking along the Purbeck Hills to

83

At Lulworth Cove a Century Back

Keats's Lulworth poem was 'Bright Star! would I were steadfast as thou art'. Hardy's poem is dated September 1920 and records what may have been his own last visit to Lulworth Cove:

Had I but lived a hundred years ago
I might have gone, as I have gone this year,
By Warmwell Cross on to a Cove I know,
And Time have placed his finger on me there:

'You see that man?' – 'I might have looked, and said,
'O yes: I see him. One that boat has brought
Which dropped down Channel round Saint Alban's
  Head.
So commonplace a youth calls not my thought.'

'You see that man?' – 'Why yes; I told you; yes:
Of an idling town-sort; thin; hair brown in hue;
And as the evening light scants less and less
He looks up at a star, as many do.'

'You see that man?' – 'Nay, leave me!' then I plead,
I have fifteen miles to vamp across the lea,
And it grows dark, and I am weary-kneed:
I have said the third time; yes, that man I see!'

'Good. That man goes to Rome – to death, despair;
And no one notes him now but you and I:
A hundred years, and the world will follow him there,
And bend with reverence where his ashes lie.'

Corfe Castle. The work at Lulworth, by Dorchester builders Wellspring & Son, was completed and consecrated on 12 May 1870.

Hardy returned to Lulwind Cove in *Far from the Madding Crowd*, written in 1873, with Sergeant Frank Troy leaving a pile of clothes on the beach in order to fake his own drowning. It was his first major literary success. The cove and Daggers Gate, thinly disguised as Dagger's Grave, also put in an appearance in *The Distracted Preacher*, a smuggling tale published in 1879. The author revisited the cove on 26 September 1881, so that his wife, Emma, could paint it.

Hardy also showed a lifelong interest in the work of John Keats. He absorbed words and images from *An Ode to a Nightingale* and paid homage to Keats in the Protestant cemetery in Rome on 21 March 1887, copying the inscription and gathering violets from the grave. He sent a couple of the flowers to friend Edmund Gosse. He told another poet, Edmund Blunden, that 'he considered it possible that John Keats on the occasion of landing at Lulworth, at the time he composed his last sonnet' went 'to visit relatives' at Broadmayne. They 'were stablemen like Keats's own father; one of them, so he

asserted, being born about 1800, being remarkably like John Keats in appearance.'

The third poet to discover Lulworth Cove was Rupert Brooke (1887–1915). At the time, in 1907, he had no idea of the Keats connection, as is shown by a letter to his mother. He did not realise the coincidence that he should lose his copy of the poet's work on the rocks at Lulworth:

One day we were reading on the rocks and I had a Keats in my pocket, and it slipped out, and, falling into a swift current, was borne out to sea. So we leapt into a boat and rowed up and down the coast till we espied it off some rocks. But the sea was rough and we could not land on that rocky part, or get near Keats. So we landed half a mile off on a beach, and came over the rock to the Keats; and when we found it, I stripped and went in after it and got it. It is indeed quite spoilt; but it only cost two shillings to begin with.

Brooke went on to write, in 1911:

Oh, I've read Keats, and found the most amazing thing. The last place he was in was Lulworth. His ship was becalmed outside. He and Severn went ashore and clambered about the rocks all day – his last fairly happy day. He went aboard and wrote, that evening, his last poem – that sonnet. The ship took him on to Italy, coughing blood and suffering hell because he wouldn't see Fanny any more. Fanny sat in Hampstead, with Mr Brown. It was at the end of September 1820.

Brooke's grandfather, Revd Richard England Brooke, lived at Grantchester Dene, 2 Littledown Road, Bournemouth. The building survives as an attachment to Dean Park Road having been cut off from the rest of the street by a relief road. Coincidentally, the house was given its name before the family moved into the home immortalised as 'The Old Vicarage at Grantchester', which is still on the fringes of English literature as the home of Jeffrey and Mary Archer.

The line of rowing boats reveals the type of craft Rupert Brooke and friends would have hired on their visits to the cove. An Edwardian paddle-steamer docks to the left.

Rupert Brooke

Soldier-poet Rupert Brooke, already nationally known, described West Lulworth as 'the most beautiful place in England'.

Rupert Brooke tired of Bournemouth and its 'decrepit and grey-haired invalids.' He wrote to his mother to tell her of his escape: '... tomorrow I'm going to the most beautiful place in the world. It is called West Lulworth.'

This destination was 'a favourite resort of the cycling community.' Although he claimed 'to do a fair amount of work here' he actually achieved less in Lulworth than he had in Bournemouth. While there he had even taken part in a political demonstration, supporting the Minority Report on Poor Law Reform. He also campaigned for 'a Compulsory Living Wage'. Away from family supervision, Brooke regarded Lulworth as a place where he could happily indulge in private pleasures. He found comparisons with Bournemouth irresistible, if only to explain his repeated absences from the family holiday home, 'no promenades, nor lifts, nor piers, nor a band.'

The attraction of Lulworth was that its Edwardian postmaster, Henry Joseph Chaffey, was ahead of his time in developing self-catering holiday apartments. Rupert heard about these from a friend and wrote to make his booking in June 1907, to reserve rooms. Friends from Cambridge were invited for what promised to be an 'hilarious' vacation with 'reading parties'. The first visit is commemorated in 'Pine-trees and the sky: Evening,' written in Lulworth, on 8 July 1907:

I'd watched the sorrow of the evening sky,
And smelt the sea, and earth, and warm clover,
And heard the waves, and the seagull's mocking cry.

And in them all was only the old cry,
That song they always sing – 'The best is over!
You may remember now, and think, and sigh,
O silly lover!'
And I was tired and sick that all was over,
And because I,
For all my thinking, never could recover
One moment of the good hours that were over.
And I was sorry and sick, and wished to die.

Then from the sad west turning wearily,
I saw the pines against the white north sky,
Very beautiful, and still, and bending over
Their sharp black heads against a quiet sky,
And there was peace in them; and I
Was happy, and forgot to play the lover,
And laughed, and did no longer wish to die;
Being glad of you, O pine trees and the sky!

'This is heaven,' he wrote from Lulworth in April 1910. 'Downs, Hens, Cottages, and the Sun.' He had said goodbye 'to the 53 little boys whose Faith and Morals I had upheld for ten weeks,' at Rugby School following the death of his father, their housemaster, and 'found I had fallen in love with them all.' In Lulworth 'escaped from the world's great snare' he read Elizabethan plays in the morning and each afternoon walked 'up perpendicular places alone for hours.'

He was a nationally reviewed poet when he returned to Lulworth for two weeks on 27 December 1911 with a 'reading party' of friends. 'There,' he told Edward Marsh, he:

... collapsed suddenly into a foodless and sleepless hell. God! how one can suffer from what my amiable specialist described as a nervous breakdown. He reported that I had got into a 'seriously introspective condition' and – more tangibly – that my weight had gone down a stone or two. I tottered, being too tired for suicide, to Cannes, not because I like the bloody place, but because my mother happened to be there.

The image of a disturbed Rupert Brooke emerges from his biography, written by Nigel Jones. Though still talented and charismatic, he was much less stable than his letters imply, with psychotic episodes and bouts of insomnia. Mood swings have him vacillating from 'loveable and randy' to 'introspective and jealous' when he behaves like 'a spoilt, self-pitying brat.' His sonnet, 'Reversed at Lulworth,' was dated 1 January 1911:

Hand trembling towards hand; the amazing lights
Of heart and eye. They stood on supreme heights.

Ah, the delirious weeks of honeymoon!
Soon they returned, and, after strange adventures,
Settled at Balham by the end of June.
Their money was in Can[adian] Pac[ific] B[ank]
Debentures
And in Antofagastus. Still he went
Cityward daily, still she did abide
At home. And both were really quite content
With work and social pleasures. Then they died
They left three children (beside George, who drank)
The eldest Jane, who married Mr Bell,
William, the head-clerk in the County Bank
And Henry, a stock-broker, doing well.

Yeats described Rupert Brooke as 'the handsomest man in England' but Leonard Woolf, husband of Virginia, regarded him as 'a professional charmer'. His companions in Dorset included the musician William Denis Browne (1888–1915), artist Albert Rutherston (1881–1953), and economist Dudley Ward (1885–1957). Ben Keeling, Duncan Grant and James Strachey are also mentioned. He looked back 'to the simplicity of the little places and quiet folks' from Harvard – met during his year in the United States – in 1913 with a chorus showing he was now equally accustomed to high society:

Would God I were eating plover's eggs,
And drinking dry champagne,

With the Bernard Shaws, Mr and Mrs Masefield, Lady Horner, Neil Primrose, Raleigh, the Right Honourable Augustine Birrell, Eddie, six or seven Asquiths, and Felicity Tree,
In Downing Street again.

Winston Churchill personally offered poet Rupert Brooke and musician Denis Browne their fateful commissions to join the Royal Naval Division at Blandford in preparation for the expedition to the Turkish-held Dardanelles for assault-landings in the Gallipoli peninsula. Edward Marsh saw them off 'excited and a little shy, like two new boys going to school – happy and handsome in their new uniforms, and specially proud of their caps.' Denis fell on 4 June 1915, bravely attacking trenches at Krithia, but Rupert was no longer at his side. He died of blood-poisoning and was buried on Friday 23 April – the day of St George and Shakespeare – on the idyllic island of Scyros. It was an olive grove, where he had sat with Denis on the Tuesday of that week, that fulfilled the lines written in Blandford Camp:

If I should die, think only this of me:
That there's some corner of a foreign field
That is for ever England. There shall be
In that rich earth a richer dust concealed;
A dust whom England bore, shaped, made aware,
Gave, once, her flowers to love, her ways to roam,
A body of England's, breathing English air,
Washed by the rivers, blest by the suns of home...

'In memory of soldiers of the Royal Armoured Corps whose ashes are scattered in this area.'
Bindon Hill, in a view southwards to Mupe Rocks.

Lest We Forget ...

The war memorial at East Lulworth, erected after the First World War, seen from the west in 2002.

The northern tablet on the War Memorial at East Lulworth, for some of those in Rupert Brooke's 'foreign field'.

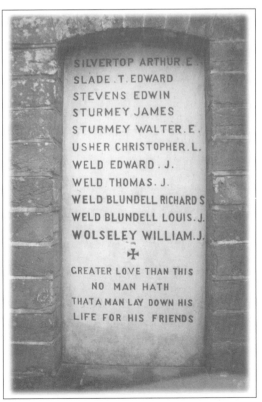

The southern tablet on the War Memorial at East Lulworth, including the Weld family contribution to the conflict.

The war memorial at West Lulworth, on the corner of Main Road and East Road,
as seen from the north-east in 2002.

War Memorials

Left: *Losses from West Lulworth in the First World War, from Budden to James, on the south side of the memorial.*

Right: *Continuing the First World War roll call of sacrifice at West Lulworth, from Legg to Webber, on the north side of the monument.*

Below: *Additional words on the south side, for Peter Elldred and John Mouland, who failed to return to West Lulworth from the Second World War.*

Tank Humour

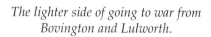

The lighter side of going to war from
Bovington and Lulworth.

Chapter 15

PHILOSOPHER'S LOVE NEST

The next national name to adopt Lulworth Cove was the distinguished mathematician, philosopher and pacifist campaigner Bertrand Russell, 3rd Earl Russell (1872–1970). He arrived in West Lulworth in 1916 as the Honourable Bertrand Arthur William Russell, brother and heir presumptive of John Francis Stanley Russell, 2nd Earl Russell (1865–1931). He had already established his scholarly reputation with a string of titles on subjects starting with *German Social Democracy* in 1896 and culminating in *Principia Mathematica*, in collaboration with old Shirburian Dr Alfred North Whitehead (1861–1947) in 1910.

That is the traditional academic introduction Russell is usually granted, which goes on to stress that he wrote dozens more books, and was awarded the ultimate accolade of the Nobel Prize for Literature in 1950. However, Lulworth people saw a

different and more revealing side of Russell, literally, as he bathed naked in the cove. Worse, from the moral standpoint, he was always in the company of undressed women, and worst of all they were a constantly changing group. Russell himself admitted he was no 'solemn stained glass saint' and 'did not respect respectable people.' Just the list of his wives makes exhausting reading and not only did the relationships overlap but past, present and future partners often shared him on holiday.

Russell's famous love nest, Newland's Farm, was shown to historian Dr Ted Ward by farmer and poet Hugh Simpson, whose collection of verse entitled *Out of Dorset* was published in 1972. Mr Simpson moved into the property in 1945. His gentrified home, with plain but graceful eighteenth-century lines, stands beside what is now the caravan camp on the landward side of Durdle Door. Russell's favourite bedroom, to

Eastern frontage of Newlands Farm in one of three photographs by Colin Graham from 1979.

Bindon Hill, looking south-eastwards from Bertrand Russell's favourite bedroom at Newlands Farm, in 1979.

which he returned at regular intervals from 1914 until 1934, looks westwards towards Bindon Hill. Russell's introduction to Newlands Farm, during the First World War, when he was a conscientious objector, came through a chance conversation with West-Lulworth shopkeeper Edward Randall. The grocer told Russell that the Watts family at the rather run-down Newlands Farm preferred bed and breakfast to dairying. They were also libertarian folks who lived a mile away from 'prudery and humbug' in the village. Randall thought the literary connection would bring more Cambridge scholars of the Rupert Brooke ilk but instead, 'weird telegrams and unusual packages' came to West Lulworth Post Office. Mrs Mitchell, who lived in East Lulworth, recalled that 'Russell and his harem had little or no contact with villagers, apart from collecting their mail.'

Russell's first marriage to Alys Whitall Pearsall Smith, in 1894, was dissolved in 1921. He became emotionally involved with Lady Ottoline Morrell, the former Lady Ottoline Cavendish-Bentinck, who was married to Liberal MP Philip Morrell, as well as a German lady, and Helen Dudley whom he had seduced on an American lecture tour. On coming out of prison, for refusing to fight in the war, Russell arranged to take Ottoline Morrell to Newlands Farm but Colette O'Neil had also captivated him. Lady Constance Malleson, who was married to

actor Miles Malleson, received similar treatment. Constance sent Bertrand red roses on his birthday for the rest of his life. They exchanged hundreds of letters and openly shared their affair in triangular relationships with husbands and mothers. Other liaisons included New Zealand author Katherine Mansfield and drug addict Vivien Eliot, who was the first wife of poet T.S. Eliot.

Dorothy Wrinch, another accomplished mathematician joined Russell's Lulworth circle. Then he married intrepid swimmer Dora Black in order to make their first child legitimate. The children, John Russell and Katherine Tait, faced a disturbed and unconventional upbringing from which they never fully recovered. To their mother, life was all about pleasure, and she justified herself by writing *The Right to be Happy*, at Lulworth in 1927. Her other lover was a Belgian artist and she delighted in 'challenging and upsetting behaviour' which left Lulworth scandalised. Her marriage to Bertrand Russell was dissolved in 1935.

That year, in August, Sir Alan Cobham dropped down at Newlands Farm as his Flying Circus moved along the coast between displays at Swanage and Weymouth. Brian O'Hare, who comes in and out of these pages as my main informant on the ground, was six years old and had little interest in wayward philosophers, but he was the first to hear the news in West Lulworth village:

Bertrand Russell

Above: *Philosopher and mathematician Bertrand Russell with prospective second wife Dora Black, who swam with him at Lulworth when they were staying at Newlands Farm.*

Above: *Russell and third wife Patricia 'Peter' Spence who also visited Lulworth, playing with son Conrad and his train set in 1940.*

Cliff-top chalets, on the brow of the hill overlooking St Oswald's Bay, were removed after the Second World War.

CHALETS ON THE HILLS ABOVE DURDLE DOOR WHICH
MUST NOW BE REMOVED

My cousins came to No. 16 with great excitement. There was an aeroplane at Newlands Farm! Tagging along with Doug, we went to see this wonder, and were rewarded at the end of the day with a free trip in the plane. The pilot had a successful day financially. Doug tried to get me to look down at Durdle Door camping site. Not likely – but I'll never forget the kindness of that pilot in giving all the O'Hares such an experience of taking off and landing in a farmer's field. I learned later that the pilot was the famous pioneer aviator Sir Alan Cobham.

Russell's third marriage, in 1936, was to Patricia 'Peter' Spence, which lasted until 1952 when he moved on to his fourth – that with Edith Finch. He first brought Peter Spence to Lulworth in 1934 and they arrived a couple of times 'with a horde of wild students.' The management of Newlands Farm changed with the arrival of A.J. Diffey. Bertrand Russell's entourage offended the expanding clientele of camp and chalet dwellers on the cliff top. Russell moved on, after the Second World War, from beach parties to peace protests; he led civil disobedience against nuclear weapons.

Cliff-top chalets, along the skyline above St Oswald's Bay, had also had their day. Removal, however, occurred in tandem with the expansion of Durdle Door Holiday Park. They were replaced with static 'vans' and a field of cars on the same viewpoint downland. Much of the oppo-

sition to the Army's occupation of the other side of Lulworth was offset by fears that tanks would make way for caravans.

Durdle Door and Portland, looking south-westwards. Photographed by Rodney Legg in 1968.

A Holiday Destination

Left: *Cars and static mobile homes now form the skyline on the downs east of Durdle Door.*

Right:
Newlands Farm seen from the south-east, between the distinctive pines of Durdle Door Holiday Park, in 1979.

Newlands Farm

Paddock view of Newlands Farm seen from the north-east, in 2000.

Right: *Rustic roofs, seen in 2000 before restoration, on barns at Newlands Farm.*

Chapter 16

EAST LULWORTH

Surviving seventeenth-century cottages opposite White Lodge Gate, almost all that is left of the original East Lulworth village. A view from the south-west in 1907.

The home village of the Weld Estate, created as the 'New Village' when Lulworth Park was being depopulated and landscaped between 1753 and 1785, East Lulworth retains an air of thatched rusticity. Now the most westerly of the buildings in the present village, a seventeenth-century cottage near the southern junction between the old main street and its bypass for tanks is a survivor from the original community.

As with the park having two churches, one Anglican and the other Catholic, the parish has two cemeteries as well. One is beside the Parish Church and the other, near the village, was created for Catholics in 1860.

Brian O'Hare, who acted as my primary informant on the two Lulworth villages in the twentieth century before the Second World War, recalled that the resident Catholic priest in East Lulworth was Father Patrick O'Reilly:

Grandma Elizabeth O'Hare insisted that the whole tribe of O'Hares attend midnight Mass at Christmas. Mass was held at East Lulworth and we would trek, toddlers and all, three miles to the church in the park in the depths of winter. We were barely able to keep our eyes open and we must have seemed like a crowd of Israelites... It was little wonder that one day I was half way up Camp Hill from Broadwall before Dad spotted me, walking alone to granny's, even though I was only three years old at the time... Walking home from church we would hurry past the Tank Park at Lulworth Camp, under the trees, as we were afraid the ghost of the Grey Lady would appear. Her face is carved into the park wall at that point.

Brian progressed from West Lulworth to the Catholic Elementary School in East Lulworth, founded by Joseph Weld in 1855 for 100 children. The mistress during the First World War was Miss Ellen Fanning.

Schools

Trees hiding most of the south-east corner of East Lulworth in 1904, looking north-west. The Elementary School may be glimpsed in the foliage (left of centre) and Elm Tree House looks positively palatial (centre).

The 1840-built Elementary School at East Lulworth, with four adults, 50 girls and boys and an elder bush in flower, as seen from the south in 1904.

Schools

Left: *The Elementary School survives, virtually unchanged, except that its name in 2002 is the Old School House.*

Below: *St Mary's House, home of the nuns who ran the Catholic School, looking south to Manor Cottage (beside car) and the Weld Arms (left) in 2002.*

Below: *St Mary's Convent School at East Lulworth, beside one of the parish's biggest oaks, seen from the north in 2002. Doug O'Hare remembers that it was a rite of passage for all the boys to climb the tree. The tall chimney held the Angelus bell which was tolled at noon every day by one of the O'Hare brothers.*

Brian remembered a number of fights whilst at school:

I used to regularly skirmish with Freddie Taylor and his brother Bertie, and the Bullimore twins, John and David, in a long-standing feud, going back to my brothers and theirs.

Nuns were running the school when Brian was born in 1929 but by the time he attended they had moved on to Bindon Abbey and Miss Yarnitsky, Miss Bellfield and Miss Brown were the teachers:

After morning prayers we did our tables in the infants' class. Those tables learnt by rote stick in the memory. There was no 'spare the rod' here and Yarny, as we called her, used the stick at her singular discretion. After all, few of the growing boys were going on to Secondary School; they would need to earn a living and go on to local workplaces. Yarny needed to keep control of those earthy, strong juveniles. The Angelus bell was still tolled at the school at midday by one of the older boys and the appropriate long prayers said by all. Yarny's treat for us was the annual summer outing when we were taken to Weymouth by coach, where we quickly spent our pocket money, had a swim, then strolled the seafront and Esplanade like the bumpkins we were. Then followed tea at a posh café with full grace at both ends. Then home to Mum and Dad. At least this gave us one over the other local schools.

The same applied at Christmas, causing a degree of jealousy, because 'we Catholic children again scored over the locals.' There would be a party especially for them, at East Lulworth, 'with modestly wished presents provided by the Welds.'

The first regular and reliable bus service was considered to be an incredible 1930s innovation for a rural backwater that had never been reached by the turnpike network. An arm of the Wareham Turnpike Trust, in operation from 1765 to 1876, headed toward East Lulworth from Holme Bridge. In three kilometres, in the middle of unfenced heathland on the eastern slope of Five Barrow Hill, a milestone offered Lulworth in two miles. In the other direction was 'London 117'.

Even after the Southern National bus service was provided between the two military complexes of Lulworth and Bovington, boys from West Lulworth did their best to miss it when it stopped beside the Weld Arms in East Lulworth, and walked the three miles home in order 'to get extra time to ourselves.' In winter, school ended at 4p.m. and the bus arrived at the Weld Arms at 4.10p.m. Summertime school hours came to an end at 3.30p.m. The boys, however, had a way of achieving 'bonus time' by advancing the clock on Yarny's desk. The same trick was in use when Sheila O'Hare, born in 1937, started school years later.

Miss Brown and Miss Yarnitsky rehearsed the children for winter plays and an annual variety show, all of which were performed in the nearby hall. Parents attended and Brian O'Hare remembered rehearsing his first song, whilst in the infants' school at the age of four, with the chorus 'the postman calls with a knock, knock, knock.' He was dressed in a postman's uniform with a hard hat lent by West-Lulworth postmaster Fred Chaffey:

I got on to the stage with my bag, looked out into the audience, and scampered as quick as I could. Yarny wasn't pleased though I was quite consoled in my tears by the older girls. A few years later I was so competent in my parts that I could carry an hour's play in the major role. Of course, once I was fighting Peter Macklin dressed as a dragon and he broke my wooden sword. Panic again but I swiftly picked up George Taylor's discarded one and 'killed' as instructed. Yarny gave me a doughnut. Miss Brown travelled to our house to teach me the piano but she gave [this] up on marrying the Welds' chauffeur.

Above: *The Weld Arms (over the right-hand door) at East Lulworth, as seen from the north in 1907. 'Edwin Bonham, Licensed to sell and retail beer, spirits and tobacco, to be consumed on the premises.'*

Above: *'Nil sine numine', the family motto on the wall of the Weld Arms, last repainted by Sandy Gordon of Wool in 1989.*

Elm Tree House

Thatched No. 24 East Lulworth, Elm Tree House, and more thatch on Nos 26, 27 and 25, looking southwards in 2002.

Chimneys of Elm Tree House as seen from the north, in a scene framed by thatch and palings. Photographed by Rodney Legg in 2002.

Dormer windows of Elm Tree House, a typical Victorian villa, which at the time of writing is the home of Stephen and Richard Levett, as seen from the east in 2002.

What a wedding present she had. They built the couple a new detached house in the castle grounds.

East Lulworth's Anglican Elementary School opened in 1840, with places for around 80 children. Its mistress during the First World War was a Mrs Greenhalgh. Churchgoers of all denominations, as well as teachers, the villagers in general and the Army worked together to make a success of the last great peacetime event at East Lulworth before war clouds gathered again. Celebrations for the Silver Jubilee of King George V in 1935 were followed by his death and the accession of King Edward VIII.

Lulworth Fête in the 1930s, featuring John O'Hare as Jack-in-the-Box, brother Doug as the fisherman, and Brian as a Red Indian.

Utilising Lulworth Park and Lulworth Castle as the setting and backdrop, with St Andrew's Parish Church as the focal point, a huge event was planned for the coronation that never happened. The village branch of the Women's Institute and teachers from the school decided to mark the holiday on 12 May 1937 with a pageant on the castle lawns. All the local WI branches were involved and it was second only to Louis Parker's Sherborne Pageant of June 1905.

In the event, the arrangements were adapted to suit the circumstances – as a result of the King's abdication, in order to marry Wallis Simpson, a twice-divorced American from Baltimore.

Post Office

Right: *The Post Office (left, now No. 6) at East Lulworth as seen from the east, in 1904. A recruitment poster for regiments of the British Army is just visible on the end of the building, and cottages No. 9 (centre) and 4 (right).*

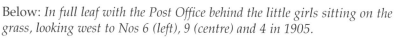

Left: *George Knight's Post Office, with a bakery at the back, looking south-eastwards towards Cockles in 1904.*

Below: *Sealed post box in the wall of what is now No. 6, East Lulworth.*

Below: *In full leaf with the Post Office behind the little girls sitting on the grass, looking west to Nos 6 (left), 9 (centre) and 4 in 1905.*

The Duke of York became King George VI. Brian O'Hare, by this time aged seven, took part in the Lulworth Pageant:

It was a glorious show. Soldiers from Lulworth Camp took the part of a Roman legion. The theme was the lovely church throughout the ages, from Ancient Britons to the Victorian parson-poet William Barnes. Because of my, well, acting prowess I was chosen to play a part with William Barnes, who overlooked the changing scenes. It was a great success, and I was spoilt by the adults, being the only child in the cast.

Born in 1929, Brian was at the safe age for a child in the 1930s, although his older brothers Ken, John and Doug left school and became Gunners. They joined the Boys' Service of the Royal Artillery at Woolwich. Ken and John became commissioned officers in the Second World War; John with the forerunners of the SAS and Doug with the Royal Horse Artillery.

The huge expansion of the Lulworth Ranges on 19 December 1943 is remembered for the evacuation and dispossession of Tyneham villagers but many around East Lulworth were also affected by orders of Winston Churchill's War Cabinet that received no coverage in local or national newspapers. Requisition orders were issued for Wareham Lodge and Mrs S.P. Damen's farmstead at The Cat on the edge of the heath beyond Black Barrow. This had a strip of land on either side of Luckford Lake, on the north side of the B3070, which heath-croppers carved out of former common land. It became a wayside inn when the well-heeled followed the fashionable royal example and took to sea-bathing in 1790. The Cat took its name from 'a big tabby cat which used to sit on the gate.'

Botany Farm, Home Farm, and landlord Edwin Bonham at the Weld Arms Inn had to give up fields.

The late-eighteenth-century hostelry has probably always carried the Weld name as it appears as such in the parish tithe assessment in 1841. As for Bonham in 1943, this was the second time he had been affected by the war. The building had an unexploded Luftwaffe bomb wedged in its thatch, which remained there until they were rediscovered and removed for detonation in 1994. Further east, in the scattered heathland hamlets around Whiteway, Povington and West Creech many lost their homes as well as the land.

The next historic estate along from Lulworth, in the Purbeck Hills but now largely incorporated into the Lulworth Ranges, belonged to the Bond family of Creech Grange and Tyneham. Both branches of the family lost land but for squire Ralph Bond and his household everything had to go. They had already handed over Tyneham House to the Royal Air Force for Brandy Bay radar station and moved to a nearby cottage. Now they lost that as well. The whole 3,003-acre Tyneham parish was evacuated. The new range boundary stopped 600 metres short of Creech Grange, which was owned by John Wentworth Garneys Bond.

Their motto 'The World is Not Enough' is attributed to Sir Thomas Bond of Peckham, who gave his name to Bond Street in 1658, in the film of that title based on Ian Fleming's character. The author went on to state in *On Her Majesty's Secret Service*, in 1963, that James Bond's 'father came from the Highlands, from near Glencoe' but acknowledged borrowing the 'non sufficit orbis' of the English Bonds from the Isle of Purbeck: 'it is an excellent motto which I shall certainly adopt.'

As for the Latin origins, although used by Juvenal in a reference to Alexander the Great, the earlier source was the poet Lucan who put the expression in the mouth of Julius Caesar, on quelling a mutiny in the ranks in the Civil Wars.

Above: 'R.J.W. 1891' date-stone with Richard Weld's initials set in the east gable of No. 44 East Lulworth.

Above: *Lone figure on the Wareham road, passing The Cat farmstead, looking south-westwards to the woods of Black Barrow in 1910.*

The Lindens

The Lindens, formerly one of the homes of the Weld family and now an out-station of Bournemouth University, at Mount Pleasant, East Lulworth. Looking eastwards from the gate in 1907.

The frontage of The Lindens, seen from the lawn to the south in 1907.

East Lulworth Homes

Above: *Gladstone bag and tabby in a delightful study of Common Hill Cottage looking south-east from the garden wall of No. 30, East Lulworth in 1907.*

Left: *The time-warp scene opposite White Lodge, comprising Nos 15 and 16 East Lulworth, in 1910.*

Right: *The cottages opposite White Lodge, still unchanged except for an extra window inserted into No. 16 East Lulworth, seen in 2001.*

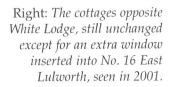

East Lulworth Homes

East Lulworth cottages, typical of those built after the eighteenth-century parkland clearances. Photographed in the 1890s.

No. 9 East Lulworth (right) and No. 4 (left), looking east towards the Coombe Keynes turning (far left) in 1907.

East Lulworth Homes

*Eighteenth-century cottage tucked into the side of Bowling Green Wood,
seen from the south-east in 2002.*

*A Tudor farmhouse, Manor Cottage, was to the east of the former village, and is now at its heart.
It is seen here from the north-east after re-thatching in 2002.*

Littlemore Cottage

Littlemore Cottage (left) and Nos 18 and 19 East Lulworth (left centre), No. 20 (centre) and gritty heath-stone-walled No. 21 (right), beside the stream from Water Barrows, looking north in 1901.

*Thatched and tile-hung Littlemore Cottage (left) and Nos 18 and 19 East Lulworth,
as seen from the south in 1907.*

Littlemore & Cockles

Right: *Littlemore Cottage (left), No. 20 East Lulworth (centre) and Cockles Cottage (with canine at gate) as seen from the south in 2002.*

Littlemore Cottage and Cockles, East Lulworth, as seen from the north-east in 2002.

Left: *The brown stone frontage of Cockles Cottage, Nos 21 and 22 East Lulworth, as seen from the west in 2002.*

Mount Pleasant

The 1793 date-stone set in the wall of No. 34 Mount Pleasant, East Lulworth.

*A range of 1793-dated cottages (Nos 30, 32, 43 and 36) at Mount Pleasant, East Lulworth,
seen from the south-west in 1900, looking along the road towards Botany Farm.*

Mount Pleasant

Right: *Nos 44, 43, 42 and 41 at the end of the Mount Pleasant cul-de-sac, East Lulworth. Viewed from the south-east in 2002.*

Left: *No. 39 Mount Pleasant, East Lulworth, as seen from the north.*

Left: *The trees of Mount Pleasant and No. 39 East Lulworth from the south in 2002.*

Right: *No. 40 Mount Pleasant, East Lulworth, looking southwards to Flower's Barrow on the skyline of the Purbeck Hills.*

Shaggs

Above: *Roadside oak dwarfing a cottage at Shaggs in 2002.*

Left: *Shaggs Cottages, forming a row of four estate houses between East Lulworth and Coombe Keynes.*

Right: *House set in Lodge Wood, west of Shaggs.*

Chapter 17

WEST LULWORTH

Activity in School Lane, in about 1905, was centred on what is now Ye Old Forge,
seen with helper Jimmy James in a view eastwards along the south side of the street to Hillside and beyond.

To John Hutchins, a couple of centuries ago, West Lulworth was a 'shabby village'. The word picturesque now comes to mind but it is fair to say it has come up in the world and some of the improvements date from relatively recent times. This account of West Lulworth in the mid-twentieth century is based on the memories of Brian O'Hare. In later life he played piano for Matt Monro and Roy Hudd in Hong Kong and retired to Ross-on-Wye. Brian O'Hare was born at No. 3 Main Road, in 1929, in the thatched cottages on the north side at Broadwall where the road enters the village from Camp Hill. The fourth son of James O'Hare and Miriam Powell, he lived there

James and Miriam 'Holly' O'Hare and their West Lulworth children, John and Ken (back row) *with Doug and Brian* (front row), *c.1935.*

with elder brothers Ken, John and Doug and younger siblings Sheila and Dennis. Perhaps the family were seen as strangers to Lulworth, Brian pondered, as they were often called 'Taffs' at school. They shared the crowded building with Toby and Dolly Harvey and their daughter Florrie, until the O'Hares were re-housed in No. 16, between the war memorial and the old churchyard.

Toby Harvey fought in the desert campaign against the Turks in Mesopotamia – breaking out of a long siege in southern Iraq – with the Dorsetshire Regiment in the First World War. The stableman for Richard Shutler at nearby Shutler's Farm, he proudly boasted: 'I can plough

Main Road

Right: The north side of the eastern part of Main Road, looking south-westwards towards the Castle Inn, in about 1900, before the felling of its oak tree and clearance of the front garden.

Left: Looking westwards along Main Road in the centre of West Lulworth, where the ancient Parish Church used to stand in the gap between the cottages, to the right of the female figure.

Right: The central length of Main Road in the 1930s, having lost some of the bucolic quaintness with the street being tarred and the telephone poles now having four tiers.

Left: Western section of Main Road in Edwardian times, looking south-westwards to Hambury Tout. No. 3 is on the right of the picture.

where they new-fangled tractors baint able to venture.'

There was a winding staircase in No. 3 and a round dormer window half-way up. A gramophone provided the family entertainment and Brian recalled brother Ken stumbling on a stair and breaking a 78-rpm record. There was relief when they found out which one: '... it wasn't Caruso singing 'O Sole Mio', which was our favourite.' By the end of the century No. 3 was the home of Margaret and Thomas Meaden.

In No. 4 Main Road lived elderly Peter Harvell and his bedridden wife. Peter showed young Brian O'Hare how to skin a rabbit:

Edwardian watercolour of the Castle Inn with a brewer's dray, pictured from the north-east.

He charged me tuppence a time for doing this and kept the skins. A van used to call regularly to collected them and paid a penny a skin. Mum cared for the invalid old woman twice a day.

Later, at Swanage Grammar School, Brian was taught by Peter's sister. No. 4 is now the home of Joan and Therese Prangnell. No. 5 Main Road was the home of Harry and Mary Hawkins with their children Doll, Bob, Tom, Peggy, Ted and John. Gerald came along later. It has since become the home of Alison Keay and Andrew Lakeman.

Next door, at the western end of the range, No. 6 was Mrs Maud Dorey's grocery store. She had two daughters, Betty and Molly, and a son, Wally. Their father had been killed in the First World War. At the start of the new millennium, No. 6 is home to Antony, Hester and Yvonne Adams.

In the thatched Castle Inn Hotel, William Alfred Dowding had the closest telephone (telephone West Lulworth 25) which was used at one time or another by most of the villagers. Hardy's Cottage was the home of Frederick Hardy, the blacksmith, whose Forge was around the corner in School Lane. Someone in the village recalled being told that the artist and illustrator William Small (1843–1929), from Worcester, once painted the scene with The Olde Malt-house, beneath a high-pitched thatched roof, facing the Castle Inn. It had a 'rig cowl swinging in the wind.'

Neat fencing beside the Castle Inn, photographed in about 1910, looking north with West Down forming the skyline above the lower section of the thatched roof.

Down from the village green, opposite the Castle Inn, lived Albert Stockley, the baker, who had also once been a farmer. His two daughters had left home to get married – to Walt Hyde and Bill Clayton – and were living in the village.

Brian O'Hare recalled the village's social activities:

There was warmth and welcome and a sticky bun sometimes. Next door the Parish Hall was a place of wonder to me in early childhood. Here were the mysteries of the Mothers' Union, Women's Institute and Whist Drives organised by the indefatigable Mrs Beale. During the winter months the villagers were diverted from sin with frequent social evenings and beetle drives. Violet Woodsford played the piano on the small stage for the Sir Roger de Coverly and Merry Widow waltz for the Valeta.

Mention of Mrs Beale and the whist drives reminds me of a couple of anecdotes. Her husband, Sid Beale, was our mobile village barber. He came around on his bike but some follicly challenged villagers seemed to receive an extraordinary number of calls. Years later I was told that he was collecting horse racing bets (there were no legal betting shops at that time). Mrs Beale used old score-cards from whist drives to write down the bids. One day she examined a card with a winning score from a previous drive. It belonged to a lady from Winfrith. Mrs Beale could see that the original pencil scores had been rubbed out and higher figures entered. What a crime! We never entertained the Winfrith lady again.

The mainstay at social evenings were the Yeates sisters – two elderly spinsters – whose brother was Thomas Yeates at Hambury Farm. They devised a 'Guess the Product' competition from picture advertisements, edited by scissors, which were pinned up around the walls of the Parish Hall. On one occasion, Ginger Meadow caused red-faced confusion by writing down the trade name of an intimate item of female personal hygiene. Wilf Wyberg accompanied songs on his mouth-organ and was often heard

Lulworth Primary School and the east end of School Lane, from the hill to the south-west.

strolling along the Main Road with his mates in the evening, treating the village to his repertoire. He was almost professional in his renditions. It was the common belief that anything was better than Harry Bennett's whistling!

Brian remembers when the hit song was Jerome Kern's 'Smoke Gets in Your Eyes', and when the introduction of traffic lights, at Bere Regis and in the great metropolis of Bournemouth, were the latest nightmare for drivers, triggering hesitation and panic attacks. He was also around to witness the formation of a youth club based at the Village Hall. Mrs Eldridge, the wife of the garage owner, called in Mr Hill, a bachelor, to teach ballroom dancing as Vi Woodsford played the piano. The boys were relieved to reach the age of graduation to the first proper Scout troop which was formed by a soldier in 1940. Bird-nesting was still socially acceptable and one of the first expeditions was to swim the lake beyond Lulworth Park to distract the swans while another stole one of their eggs, from a wild place teeming with adders and aquatic grass-snakes.

Brian O'Hare resumes his story:

There was no electricity supply until 1937. At home we used paraffin lamps and a battery wireless, as did almost all of the village. When there was to be an events evening in the Parish Hall, Dad used to run the generator in order to charge up the batteries to provide electric light. We looked forward to the Christmas party, meeting there at 3p.m. with our own spoons for the jelly, after having to negotiate the road, which was covered with cow muck, where the cattle were led to the fields each day.

Percy Wellstead's shop was in an old hut dating back to the First World War, erected at the foot of the slope opposite the Castle Inn. It faced the junction of School Lane and Main Road and stocked drapery and haberdashery. Opening hours were restricted to one day a week.

There was a covered village well beside No. 17 Main Road and the next tap for communal use was at No. 14. Here Brian O'Hare had his earliest memory of 'waiting in the cold with Mum.' Repeat visits had to be made for water for a bath in front of the fire. Georgie Hawkins lived with his wife and sons Wilf, Steve and Cis in this cottage. It was whilst playing with old farm machinery in the nearby Barton that Cis Hawkins caught his hand in the cogs and lost a finger. 'You could hear his screams for miles,' Brian was told.

Weld estate worker Alfred Haimes, who moved into Wilton Cottage in School Lane, was in charge of the water-pumping station toward the cove.

Another estate worker, Harry Bennett, married to a member of the Sartin family from Coombe Keynes, moved into No. 15 and was in charge of Newlands Caravan Camp. 'Harry whistled the latest songs endlessly and worked from dawn to dusk,' Brian recalled.

He made a beautiful garden. Mum used to creep round and pinch cuttings until one day she found a wide-eyed

School Lane

Left: *The Olde Malt-house in School Lane, seen from the west.*

Right: *School Lane, eastwards towards Ye Olde Forge (left of centre).*

Wilton Cottage, School Lane, from the south-east. After the demise of Miss Wilton and her stray cats, it was the home of Alfred Haimes, operator of the village water pump.

Mrs Bennett at her shoulder. The Bennetts had a baby, Mavis, around the same time Mum had Sheila. Mavis Bennett caught meningitis and was deaf as a result. A retired nurse, Miss Dunning, came as a live-in carer. When Mavis went to a special school in Exeter, Miss Dunning opened a sweet and ladies shop in the old shoe-repair shop. Mum was dismayed by this, but in time we all came to accept life as it was, with little regret. Harry was the kindest neighbour ever. He would show me gardening skills, and do-it-yourself, and electric wiring was simplicity to him. Mavis picked up songs I played by lip-reading and Sheila was able to make Mavis understand anything.

Reg Norris, living in No. 17, cut roadside verges for Dorset County Council. He married Miss Wellstead, a schoolteacher.

Sergeant Ernest Catchpole lived with his wife and daughter, Georgina, in No. 18. Although he never mentioned the fact to villagers, Corporal Catchpole, as he was at the time, was the first on the scene when Lawrence of Arabia sustained fatal injuries in his motorcycle crash between Bovington and Clouds Hill at 11.30a.m. on Monday 13 May 1935. Catchpole told the inquest about a black car, passing Lawrence from the other direction, which was never traced. Colonel Thomas Edward Lawrence, riding his Brough Superior, had hit a boy cyclist.

L.M. Foot, who served with Catchpole in the Ordnance Corps, told me about the strange sequel:

Catchpole ended his own life in Egypt between June and September 1940, the reason for which still confounds me, and further adds to the Lawrence saga.

I took over the Senior NCO's bunk or quarter in which Catchpole met his end and many a time I lay looking at the bullet hole in the ceiling wondering what made him do such a thing and thinking it was the last link with the Lawrence incident.

In No. 19, Albert Spavins was the newly appointed NAAFI manager, at Lulworth Camp. Highway labourer Jonah Whittle lived with his wife and daughters, Joy, Mary and Daisy, in No. 20, opposite the war memorial, which is now the home of Ian and Margaret Davies. Mrs Cissie O'Hare was the proprietress of Bishop's Cottage Guest House (West Lulworth 32). Married to Brian's uncle Cecil she was the mother of Patrick, Peggy, Peter, Betty and Donald.

Behind the cottages the toilets were communal facilities from another age. Not only were they at the ends of the gardens but some villagers shared access to them and had to go through a neighbour's front door to reach them. For most of these humble dwellings the Weld family charged one shilling and sixpence per week, which was payable to a burly Scotsman, Ian Somerled MacDonald, agent to the Lulworth Castle estate (West Lulworth 63). He lived in the Grey House in East Lulworth.

The Elementary School, at the end of School Lane turning opposite the Castle Inn, was built in 1862 for 80 children. The house for the mistress was adjoining, and Miss Emma Eckett filled this role during the First World War. A generation later, at the start of the next conflict, headmistress Miss French belted out Sir Edward Elgar's 'Pomp and Circumstance' on the piano at assembly, whenever there was uplifting war news to be announced.

Edwardian view of Churchfield House (right), the former Red Lion Inn, looking west along West Road.

Weston, Oswald and Anchor House on the scrubby cliffs towards Dungy Head.

Above: *St Patrick's (top right) and Sycamore Villas, (top left) in a view north-westwards towards West Down in about 1905.*

'What a glorious start to a school day, having to splash through the cow slurry into that manure-ridden road,' Brian O'Hare said, though he was spared the experience of having to walk to East Lulworth instead:

The state of the road was even worse than the home of the Victorian-dressed Miss Wilton who lived in Wilton Cottage. It was a beautiful house but surrounded by hordes of stray cats. I went in once on an errand. Never again!

Old Woodsford was the patriarch of School Lane and the principal rabbit-catcher from Newlands Warren to Lulworth Camp:

The furze fields towards Newlands Farm in the lea of Hambury Tout were teeming with rabbits, and there were several established warrens on the road to Winfrith. Old man Woodsford passed through the village on his bicycle each day, both shoulders strung with rabbits. He sold the skins for coney-fur to a city trader, and the paunched rabbit carcasses to a commercial butcher. This was a business that ended with him, as wartime intensive ploughing was followed by the myxomatosis epidemic. Another traditional trade had been extinguished and the warrens are long since gone.

Another West-Lulworth character of the 1930s was Bill Wyberg who rode a dilapidated motorcycle and sidecar combination, illuminated by carbide lamps, which served as emergency transport for villagers. Mobility was becoming a necessity. The clouds of war brought full employment, both locally at Lulworth Camp, and across the Frome valley at the new military Warmwell Aerodrome. Many villagers also found work at the Royal Naval cordite factory, which produced the firing propellant for shells, on Holton Heath.

Soon the whole of the front-line Dorset coast had Defence Area status and emergency passports had to be shown at roadblocks and on buses. The first Southern National bus service in the village linked West Lulworth and Lulworth Camp with its counterpart civilian and military communities at Wool and Bovington. It ran twice a day. As the war started, the last summer holiday-makers were on the way home, the Saturday before Sunday 3 September 1939. There was now a new local industry in the rooms that became vacant, as young men went to war. Others arrived and required bed and breakfast (initially 3 shillings 6 pence a night). These were single men. They were both in and out of uniform and locals did not ask why they were there. All were connected with Lulworth Camp or involved in other secret work. The first villager to lose his life in the conflict was Peter Eldridge who enlisted in the Royal Air Force in April 1939.

Victorian and Edwardian villas towards the seaside end of the village included the Shirley Guest House run by Mr and Mrs W.R. Elldred (West Lulworth 40). Their 'modern and convenient accommodation' boasted 'hot and cold water in all bedrooms' and garaging for 20 cars. Henry Thompson, the local builder, lived in Sycamore Villa. Percy Wellstead, a draper from Wareham, was the other tradesman.

Henry Joseph Chaffey ran the Post Office, its post-round, and stationery shop (West Lulworth 20 and 68). He was succeeded by Alf Chaffey. Bill Chaffey had the coal-yard. The family also ran holiday apartments. The village's other grocery shop, Boon's Stores (West Lulworth 29), joined with Mrs Dorey in refusing to stock cigarettes. They were sold in public houses and

Football Winners

Triumphant outside the Castle Inn, West Lulworth, c.1935.
Left to right, back row: Les Charles, Pat O'Hare, Les Prentice;
centre: Ken O'Hare, Viv Hardy, Clarence Ellis;
front row: Don Dowding, George Hawkins, Wilf Hawkins, Doug O'Hare and John O'Hare.

Lulworth Ancient Order of Foresters Football Team, mid-1930s.

the beach shops in summer but most of the villagers bought their tobacco from Mrs Stockley and her sister Miss Wilbert in a cottage near the Parish Hall. Brian O'Hare was a regular buyer, on behalf of his father, whose favourite was a packet of Star cigarettes.

Churchfield House, the old Red Lion Inn in West Road where playwright John O'Keeffe found his John Barleycorn, was a guest house run by Mrs Lovell. Reginald Lovell was secretary of the British Legion Club. Churchfield is now the home of Diane, Leon and Patrick Coade.

Tewkesbury Cottage, which I understood was once owned by Tewkesbury Abbey, apparently takes its name from being 'the holiday home of a Bishop of Tewkesbury.' In any event it has been neatly re-roofed by Rod Miller, Lulworth's own thatcher, who lives in Belhuish Valley. In the first years of the twenty-first century, it is the home of Jackie Lang who joined in the debate on the relative merits of reed and wheat in traditional roofing – of which more later. ('Why would you want straw when reed has to be better? You can't afford to re-roof once you retire so you want a roof to last a lifetime.')

Surrounding land was farmed by A.J. Diffey from Newlands Farm, and Henry Mouland, after the death of the wonderfully named Obadiah Legg, in 1912. Thomas Yeates lived down in the dip, between West Lulworth village and Lulworth Cove hamlet, dairying at Hambury Farm. He could speak pure Dorset and was well-versed in local folklore and dialect sayings.

The Old Farmhouse in Farm Lane.

'Old Joe' had the horse-drawn milk round and owned the field where the local lads played football. The field was the setting for a number of fights between local gangs to establish ownership; on one particular occasion the brothers John and Gerald Hawkins along with their nephew Ken Williamson took on the might of the Meaden and Angliss tribes in the Battle of Joe's Plot. Weaponry included sticks, stones and mud pies.

Well-heeled residents complete the picture. Hugo Friedlander was at The Lynches, at the end of West Road, opposite the Parish Church. He was associated with West End actress Dorothy Dickson who used it as a holiday home and hosted a series of wild parties there. She took on the mantle of Bertrand Russell in offending village morals. Famous socialites were in her circle, and they brought to West Lulworth the shock revelation that had already been exposed in American newspapers – that the new King Edward, who was unmarried at 42 years old, and divorcee Mrs Wallis Simpson were romantically involved.

Colonel and Mrs Henry Denne Robson lived in a viewpoint villa, Oswald, beside Britwell Drive. This is the private road leading from the Lulworth Cove to Dungy Head. It is now the home of Anne and David Dickson. Cyril Rhodes and his family lived at Hambury Bottom, where Elizabeth Rudd also now lives at the time of writing.

Sir Alfred Downing Fripp (1865–1930) lived at Bindon Waters. Born in Blandford, he was Surgeon in Ordinary to King Edward VII, and to the Duke of Connaught. With Sir Frederick Treves, from Dorchester, he was one of the two Dorset surgeons who attended Edward VII. It was in Sir Alfred's absence, during the Boer War as chief civilian medical officer in the Imperial Yeomanry Hospital in South Africa, that Treves famously stepped into the breach. The King needed an operation for appendicitis but was determined not to go into hospital. 'I have a coronation on hand,' he said. 'It will be a funeral, if you don't have the operation,' Treves replied. The King capitulated. Although Treves intended to remove the appendix, he decided on the operating table to vary the appendicectomy; an abscess was drained but the appendix was left in place. The King soon recovered and his delayed coronation took place in June 1902. Treves later wrote a manuscript about the pioneering operation but it was suppressed.

His friend, Sir Alfred Fripp, never achieved such a high profile but nevertheless carried out many operations, working for years in Guy's Hospital in London. Bindon Waters was re-named Weston by Lady Fripp and is now the residence of Benedict and Valerie Hargreaves.

Captain F. Godfrey Shreiber was living in Stair House, which is now the home of Barbara and Felicity Redman. Mrs Hervey was at Grafton Lodge and the Misses Yeates were at Mellstock. Revd Christopher Campbell Sharpe was at the vicarage where his successor, Revd William Rogers now abides.

Barrister and mountaineer Sir Claud Schuster, 1st Baron Schuster (1869–1956), lived at Gatton Cottage. He was Permanent Secretary to the Lord Chancellor from 1915 to 1944 and post-war legal director of the British section of the Allied Commission for Austria.

Burngate Farm, up the hill from Lulworth Camp, was still a working farm run by Dougal Williamson (West Lulworth 35). At the time of writing it is the home of retired General Sir Michael Palmer (born 1928) and Lady Jillean Palmer, née Sherston. General Palmer was Assistant Chief of Staff, Allied Forces Central Europe, during the Cold War. He was appointed Director of the Royal Armoured Corps in 1978.

Above: *The linking ribbon of buildings between West Lulworth village and Lulworth Cove hamlet, as seen from the west in 1995, towards the skyline of Bindon Hill.*

Left: *Linking thatch between West Lulworth and Lulworth Cove hamlet, on an older raised length of the Main Road. Formerly the home of the Stevens family, seen from the south in 1997.*

Chapter 18

LULWORTH COVE

General view of Lulworth Cove and its hamlet, looking south-eastwards from Hambury Tout, over a car park – remarkable for having only two cars when Rodney Legg took the photograph in 1971.

The miracle fall took place at Lulworth Cove on 7 September 1892. Sir Frederick Treves, the Dorchester-born surgeon to Edward VII who drained the King's appendix and befriended 'Elephant Man' Joseph Merrick, was called by the coastguard to attend a girl who had fallen the 380-feet entirety of the virtually vertical side of Bindon Hill. Somehow she had slipped and bounced from the grass to the pebbles without incurring any permanent injuries. Oddly, Treves recalled, at the moment it happened he was reading a book by the girl's father who was neither known to him nor in Lulworth at the time.

Empress, from Weymouth, beached and about to unload on a busy day in 1948.

Much less significant, in terms of the distance

dropped, Tyrell Beale fell from the landing stage when he was a small child. For years afterwards he proudly displayed extensive scarring on his upper leg to other boys as they sunbathed on the beach.

The landing stage saw its busiest days when various paddle-steamers arrived from Weymouth, Swanage and Bournemouth and disgorged hundreds of visitors at a time. Boats came in bow first and reversed out on a straight course, entering and leaving east of centre at the cove entrance. Cosens & Co. from Weymouth were the principal operators through to when the service ended in 1962 (although it was not in operation during the wars). Bournemouth's

123

Evening Echo reported the absence of sailings in 1963:

Consul, *Britain's oldest paddle-steamer, has ploughed the seas from Weymouth to Bournemouth since 1897. But she has been losing money for the past two years and her owners, Cosens & Co., are to lay her up in Weymouth. This year, for the first time in living memory, there will be no paddle-steamer trips to Lulworth Cove.*

In fact the service was also absent from 1940 to 1948, when paddle-steamers were requisitioned for use as auxiliary minesweepers and wreck-clearance work. They also took battle honours and casualties in the Dunkirk evacuation. A post-war Government provided a replacement for one of those losses; the PS *Waverley* often makes nostalgic returns to the Dorset coast for the Paddle-Steamer Preservation Trust.

Among the state of the art leisure boats that used to put into Lulworth Cove were Teal-type racing yachts including the 23-metre *Shamrock* and *St Patrick*. They were owned by tea-plantation owner Sir Thomas Johnstone Lipton (1850–1931). He flew the pennant of the Royal Dorset Yacht Club below that of the Royal Yacht Squadron with another ten clubs between them.

Cecil O'Hare, uncle of Brian and Doug, 'spent many thousands of hours in his company.' One night, the *Girl Pat*, another large yacht, berthed at Lulworth. It was rumoured that Cecil had been taken on as deck-hand and departed for the Mediterranean. Doug takes up the story:

Several months later the English national press reported the craft missing, believed sunk off Tangier. There were rumours of it being engaged in smuggling between Africa and Europe and [it being] on the 'wanted' list of the International Customs Authority. It was reported found but I cannot remember the final outcome. Significantly, Cecil wasn't seen in Lulworth until many months later, and although he never had any money somehow he bought the Brooke Williams boat business a little later.

The southern boathouse at Lulworth Cove with Smooth Talker *about to slip its tongue. Photographed by Rodney Legg in 1995.*

The beach (including its landing stage, boat-hire business, fishing boats and lobster pots) was the domain of Brooke Williams and brothers Charles and John Miller. Mrs Nathaniel Miller and Mrs Phoebe Hartell each ran refreshment rooms. They all faced impossible competition when the great shoals of mackerel were being seine-netted in their thousands on the Chesil Beach. 'Weymouth mackerel,' the itinerant fishmonger shouted, as fish were offered in bulk at a price that could not be matched on the Lulworth Grounds.

Avalon Collard was the Victorian landlord of Lulworth Cove Hotel and was followed by Mrs Sarah Caveen in Edwardian times. By the 1930s, Miss E.E. Plumb was the landlady at the Cove Hotel and Restaurant (West Lulworth 23) which passed by marriage into the Ennis family. Their porter, Johnny Meaden, drove a ramshackle bus which provided the local public transport. The Ennis tribe were staunch Catholics and the bus took them to Bindon Abbey where Father Prior conducted Sunday Mass as well as Corpus Christi processions for the nuns. The bus was almost filled with two branches of O'Hares (children of brothers Cecil and

Tacky beach hut and the fishermen's ghetto, replete with vintage car, looking south-east to the western side of the entrance of Lulworth Cove before the First World War.

Edwardian entrance to Lulworth Cove with the centre building (behind trees) being the Post Office, looking west with the Cove Hotel in the foreground.

James) and became overloaded with the arrival of Daisy Whittle, Amy James and the Clark family in the village. Eventually a church was provided locally in response to their petitions and Father Prior made Lulworth Cove his priority.

Lulworth Cove was the O'Hare holiday haunt:

We were always on the beach and roamed the rocks with Albert Spavins, who had moved to Sunnyside, or Richard Shutler when he was home from boarding school. We fished with limpet for blennies and, in time, with ragwort for wrasse. Richard's mother ran a café on the beach in holiday time and that was where I drank my first cup of coffee. We went to his father's fields to pick a young, tender swede to peel and eat raw as we explored. Both of us searched for discarded beer bottles, which we took to the Cove Hotel for the half-penny deposit payable on their return. Provided they matched the hotel's stock we could have enough to buy fish-hooks at the Post Office. Richard Shutler and his sister, Jennifer, were both given rowing boats. Then we graduated to mackerel fishing with spinners from the

boat. That meant more foraging for beer bottles when the spinners were lost.

Bernard Cracroft was living in the Mill House where Stephen Brockway now has the Mill House Hotel. The Hazard Private Hotel at Lulworth Cove was owned by John Wilson-Claridge (West Lulworth 10). Thomas Edward Williams was the local motor mechanic (West Lulworth 26).

Cove Cottage is a Georgian cottage orné complete with rustic-fashion thatched roof. Spring Cottage, towards the seaside end of the hamlet, features early-Victorian brick and thatch, with a fashionable veranda and French windows.

Up the road lies stone-roofed Doll's House. This is a miniature eighteenth-century cottage, with only its fireplace and chimney built to what we would consider real size. Tiny cottages such as this one used to be commonplace, although seldom quite this small, and most came in twos or threes that have since been knocked into a single dwelling. This one is a rarity in that it has never been extended. It now plays its part in the

Spring Cottage, looking more rustic than intended with corrugated iron on its Georgian veranda, as seen from the south-west in 1997.

Mill House Hotel

Left: *Looking northwards across the former Mill Pond to Mill House Hotel, c.1955.*

Right: *A closer view of Mill House Hotel from what is now the duck pond.*

Cottages

The Doll's House, now a fishing museum. Photographed by Colin Graham in 1984.

The long Victorian frontage of the Coastguard Cottages, looking south-west across the Mill Pond. Photographed by Colin Graham in 1983.

The Coastguard Cottages, from the south-west in 1998, with Cove Cottage beyond (left) and Bindon Hill rising above.

Cove Cottage

Cove Cottage, dating from about 1760, is the 'cottage orné' beside the cul-de-sac down to Lulworth Cove, in a view looking north, 1920.

Gothic sun and shadow, in an intimate view of Georgian rustic-style Cove Cottage, photographed by David Popham in 1965.

Cove Cottage, with pines above on Bindon Hill, seen from the west in 1997.

heritage industry as the local fishing museum. It includes one room downstairs with two smaller bedrooms upstairs.

Opposite Mill House Hotel, overlooking the Mill Pond, the Coastguard Station was still operational during the First World War. Its chief officer, Charles Gennings, had a staff of seven men. They manned the Lookout, otherwise known as Nelson Fort, above the eastern entrance to the cove. It was in use for more than a century – from the Napoleonic Wars to the First World War – in order to register movements of the fleet.

The local hero at Lulworth Cove for the entirety of the second half of the twentieth century was Gerald Plant (1918–99). Known as 'Yo-Yo', for the way he bounced up and down the cliffs on a rope to rescue misadventurous climbers, he died in retirement at Corfe Castle only days away from the new millennium. The Plant family lived in Whiteway hamlet, which was absorbed into the Lulworth Ranges in 1943. Gerry Plant led the cliff-rescue team at West Lulworth, between 1947 and 1984.

He was awarded the British Empire Medal for life-saving numerous times, including a daring mission in which he descended from Worbarrow Tout to rescue a person trapped in a cave. He then successfully hauled and propelled him into the Swanage Lifeboat 'as it tipped about like a cork.' Gerry remembered:

Looking out over the car park at Lulworth Cove, the assertive lines of Cromwell House Hotel, with wrought-iron balconies linking the three-storey bay windows. Photographed from the west in 1997.

The storeman at Lulworth Camp, he was quite impressed by my free-climbing. There was a winchman descending from a Wessex helicopter, as its rotor blades came within inches of a rocky cliff above Lulworth Cove, a shudder away from coming down on both of us. I just carried on climbing, as the engine noise and down-draught made conversation impossible.

Gerry gave me a word of advice, which came in useful years later, to quell hysterics on the ground as I accomplished a similar hairy climb, plus leap, to catch lost cat Silvester in a Portland quarry, 'tell them you are a mountaineer.'

Rock-climbing was just one rite of passage which had to be achieved before wearing long trousers. The other was 'to swim the cove.' In Brian O'Hare's time, when he and cousin Betty crossed the water and came back, the next objective was to climb the cliffs and collect seagull eggs just like Weld-estate thatcher Mr Lockyer could do '... with little fear but with a good element of safety and self-preservation.' There were occasional casualties and then a tragedy. Ken Williamson climbed Stair Hole with his pal Rex Shutler. Rex came back alone. Ken had fallen; his body was washed up at Durdle Door a week later.

The turning area at the north end of the cove cul-de-sac is overlooked by Cromwell House Hotel. Flamboyant and tall, graced with ironwork and balconies, this is the perfect example of late-Victorian hotel architecture on the Dorset coast. It was whilst staying here in September 1923 that Revd James Owen Hannay (1865–1950) began writing the novel, *Bindon Parva*. It is about a Purbeck parson who celebrates communion with his dead parishioners, an unseen congregation of all classes who span the centuries and whose lives and doings he feels are absorbed into the very fabric of the building. Hannay was at that time the chaplain to the British community in Budapest. On returning to Britain permanently, he became rector of Mells, Somerset, from 1924 to 1935. He published *Bindon Parva* in 1925 under the pseudonym George A. Birmingham.

Across the water, on the other side of the cove, lived Sir Lionel Pepler (1882–1959) who gives his name to Pepler's Point which overlooks the eastern side of the entrance. For half a century he rented Little Bindon, beside the site of the original Bindon Abbey, as a holiday and retirement home. There he indulged in his great passion – to have a good bonfire as he held back acres of bramble bushes in what was virtually his own private valley. From his base at 49 Rivermead Court, Hurlingham, London SW6 he became the guru of the urban jungle. Not only did he lay out great estates but as early as 1914 he mapped the forerunner of the motorway system with arterial roads, work that resulted from a series of conferences he organised.

Between the wars Pepler consolidated his reputation as Britain's leading town planner as he changed the focus of his work from slums to aviation; the Unhealthy Areas Committee was followed by the Aerodromes Advisory Board. From 1919–41 he was Chief Town Planning Inspector at the Ministry of Health. He then chaired the inter-Allied committee looking forward to post-war Physical Planning and Reconstruction. He drafted the Town and County Planning Act and was rewarded with a knighthood in 1948. Then he helped organise the Festival of Britain, rebuild and expand Singapore, and received the first gold medal awarded by the Town Planning Institute.

All of this may have helped Dorset to stay on the fringes of the new world order. On the exposed headland a stone seat stands as his memorial with plenty of words to tell us how he 'loved the land of England' with 'Dorset best of all.' None reveals that he was Britain's foremost town planner. I wonder why.

Sir Lionel Pepler's cottage at Little Bindon, photographed by Colin Graham in 1984. Looking south-westwards from the site of Bindon Abbey.

Lulworth Cove and its car park, looking eastwards to Bindon Hill and St Alban's Head (far right).

The Hamlet

Right: *The centre of Lulworth Cove hamlet in the 1930s, looking north-west from above the pumping station to Mill House Hotel (centre) and Bishop's Cottage (right).*

Left: *Lulworth Cove hamlet, looking north-east from above the Coastguard Cottages (left) and Mill House, to adventurous attempt at landscaping above the seaward villas in 1900.*

Right: *The inner cove and hamlet, in the 1930s, looking south-east from above the Coastguard Cottages and Britwell Drive.*

Left: *View westwards from the cove hamlet in 1955, from above the thatched roofs of Spring Cottage and Cove Cottage to the Post Office and rebuilt Cove Hotel with Britwell Drive and the path to Durdle Door rising beyond.*

Chapter 19

LULWORTH CAMP

One of the earliest of the county's photographs, from July 1864, appropriately showing the Army in position above Lulworth Cove, with the Dorset Rifle Volunteers at their summer camp above the present car park in a view looking south-east.

Lulworth Cove has been popular with the Armed Forces since Victorian times. Seaside summer camps for Militia and Yeomanry volunteers were held in what is now the car park. The machines of the future arrived in the stalemate period of the First World War after a series of trenches, replicating a section of the Western Front, had been dug across the northern slopes of Gallows Hill, between Bovington and Bere Regis. The encampment at St Andrew's Farm, West Lulworth, was established to enable live-fire gunnery practice, on Bindon Hill where the sea provided a safe overshoot zone. Booms, explosions and machine-gun fire have been commonplace around Lulworth, both day and night, for

Line-up of some 25 early tanks, facing westwards for a gunnery exercise below Bindon Hill, in a view looking north-east to the woods of Gatemerston and Lulworth Park.

the whole of living memory. Even before that, it provided the subject for a Thomas Hardy poem, as the sound of 'Channel firing' has long echoed against the line of coastal hills from the Royal Navy's offshore danger area.

The Heavy Branch of the Machine-Gun Corps moved to Dorset from Canada Farm, Elvedon, near Thetford, in December 1916. The concept of an armoured fighting vehicle on caterpillar tracks had been pressed upon a reluctant War Office by Lieutenant-Colonel Ernest Swinton who was serving as a war correspondent rather than as a soldier and had stretched his credibility still further by writing fiction under the pseudonym Backside Forethought.

Tanks facing east in a view from the north-west, looking towards the inland flank of Bindon Hill.

By December 1916 tank crews were being trained at Bovington and Lulworth as tanks went into action on the Western Front.

Swinton persevered at the next offices in Whitehall, calling at the Admiralty where he had a more sympathetic hearing from a fellow war correspondent, Winston Churchill MP, as First Lord of the Admiralty. Never at a loss for a suitable sounding name, and to disguise something of no earthly relevance to his department, Churchill formed a Landships Committee.

Nautical names for the tortoise-like vehicle progressed from hull, through cistern, to tank. The Army came back into the picture after William

Tritton met Major W.G. Wilson in the White Hart Hotel, Lincoln, in September 1915 and conceived 'the first fighting tank' which resulted in the box-like No. 1 Lincoln Machine. This evolved into a modified version called Little Willie, which had more efficient tracks.

King George V brought royal patronage when he rode around the grounds of Lord Salisbury's Hatfield Park in a tank on 8 February 1916. To make the course a little more taxing a ten-feet trench had been dug and a four-feet vertical obstacle prepared.

Below: *A Mark V heavy tank from the First World War on an excursion from the Tank Museum to the Heath Range at Lulworth where it posed beside the then current main battle tank, the Chieftain, in the 1970s.*

Above: *Tents and the first tanks below Bindon Hill in a view northwards towards St Andrew's Farm, 1918.*

The tank cleared both and impressed virtually everyone except Lord Kitchener. 'A pretty mechanical toy,' he barked, after it had left the crew semi-conscious in the operation.

The King, however, knew a good toy when he saw one and suggested the Army order the first batch of tanks. Colonel Swinton was given command of the new Tank Detachment at Siberia Farm, Bisley Camp, Surrey, on 16 February 1916. It was renamed the Armoured Car Section of the Motor Machine-Gun Corps in March 1916, to restore a degree of secrecy. This was then changed to the Heavy Section of the Machine-Gun Corps in May 1916. Heavy Section was renamed Heavy Branch on 16 November 1916 and that was its name when advance parties of the Machine-Gun Corps arrived in Dorset.

The tank provoked mixed reactions when it reached the Western Front. Major-General John Fuller thought it was 'a graceful machine with beautiful lines' which would become 'an armoured mechanical horse.' Of the first 100 tanks, 49 went into action on 15 September 1916. The actions of three, from D-Company of the Tank Corps, achieved a moment of historical significance, which was witnessed from the air. 'A tank is walking up the High Street of Flers with the British Army cheering behind.'

The Tank Corps was adopted by a war artist, Solomon Joseph Solomon RA (1860–1927). He was a fashionable portrait painter, attached to the Royal Engineers. He set to work with stencils on the new war machines as they stood in sidings on flat-bed railway wagons. Across the front-plate between the caterpillar tracks, he emblazoned them with 'HMLS', which stood for His Majesty's Land Ship, as well as the name of the tank, and individual flourishes 'like the figureheads on wooden warships.' Other messages such as 'With care to Petrograd' were stencilled on the sides. 'Inscrutable Chinese eyes' featured as the camouflage on Diana, a Mark V, which was chosen from many post-war hulks in the Tank Park at Bovington to be set on stones on the corner of Somme Road and Swinton Road.

Nelson Thomson, a Purbeck quarryman who retired to Langton Matravers, remembered them well and looked back to 1916, when he was a young shepherd for Alan Budden of Burngate Farm, West Lulworth, as he talked to me in 1971:

When they used to bring the tanks over from Bovington they used to shut us behind screens of hurdles or take us away so that we couldn't see them. They put an Army control all along the roads and if anybody was within sight they used to put them off. It didn't make any difference, because, when we were at Lulworth, the tanks was going along the road and firing there – and we was watching them.

What I used to have to do was to take the sheep down on to the range from five o'clock to nine o'clock in the morning and then they started firing and I had to bring them back. Then at two o'clock I'd bring them down, some days, from two to three o'clock, and then back again. And then from six o'clock to eight o'clock in the evening. One time there I can remember a military policeman came out and started chasing me. I had sheep and troops and everything all mixed up together out of the square, opposite from where their tanks was.

When Lulworth Camp started it was all tents. They were sleeping under canvas. I can remember when the Post Office at Lulworth got hit with a shell. I don't know whether it was 1916 but there was an awful disturbance about it. Two shells went adrift somewhere – they said they ricocheted – and the Post Office and one of the houses got hit. The shells came from the tanks on the tank range at Lulworth.

Taking over St Andrew's Farm from what has become Lulworth Camp was a secret military operation which took the occupants by surprise. The Weld estate may have received prior notification but no one passed this on to the farming tenants. 'We had very short notice to get out from there,' Nelson Thomson remembered. 'It was 12 o'clock midnight when we went away from that farm and went down to Coombe Keynes to a man named Mr Ford.'

The Heavy Branch of the Machine-Gun Corps was renamed the Tank Corps on 28 July 1917 and had its greatest success on 19 August 1917. The decision had been taken to knock out a string of German pill-boxes at St Julien. Their walls were made of reinforced concrete, a metre thick, and the High Command estimated it would cost 1,000 British casualties. Instead, in a departure from usual practice, the tanks advanced first without any preliminary bombardment. Infantry followed under a smoke screen. There were only two British deaths.

On 20 November 1917 Brigadier-General Hugh Elles, at the Western Front in Hilda – flying the new Tank Corps banner from an ash stick – led a massed force of 350 tanks. They smashed through every line of trenches in the German front. It was the first time this had been achieved since the stalemate of trench warfare had extended across Europe. The War Office had estimated that such a breakthrough would take five months and require a total of £20 million of ammunition. As a result no infantry had been allocated for the offensive. No one followed through the breach.

There followed a great British cover up. In this the War Office had more talent than they ever showed for fighting. They excelled themselves and invented a German hero who had halted the advance. Never before had the British press been allowed to admit that there were any brave Germans. Yet here they were issued with the story of a mythical man:

I came to a German field battery, every gun out of action except one. By this was lying a single German officer, quite dead. In front of him were five tanks which he had evidently succeeded in knocking out single-handed with his gun. A brave man.

It was a story that was put forward by reactionaries for the rest of the war, as a reason for abandoning the tank building programme, but the tank was now its own justification. By the end of the war the Germans had their own tanks and the British line was broken wherever they attacked. The French also had their tanks though Fuller was unimpressed by 'a kind of kitchen range on tracks, unblushingly useless.' British tanks won the decisive battle of the First World War on 8 August 1918 when they tore a gap 11 miles wide through the German lines. The Kaiser said that evening, 'it is very strange that our men cannot get used to tanks.'

A German historian credited the Allied victory to 'General Tank'. The British Commander-in-Chief agreed. General Sir Douglas Haig praised the tanks for bringing about the Armistice:

Since the opening of our offensive on 8 August tanks have been employed in every battle and the importance of the part played by them in breaking the resistance of German infantry can scarcely be exaggerated.

In their two years in action, the Tank Corps led by General Elles had suffered losses of 879 dead, 935 missing and 5,302 wounded. They won four Victoria Cross citations for valour in the face of the enemy. The first went to Captain Clement Robertson who led his tanks of A-Battalion on foot, in order to navigate them through difficult terrain near Polygon Wood, Reutel, and 'deliberately sacrificed his life to make certain the success of his tanks' in the third Battle of Ypres on 4 October 1917.

Captain Richard William Leslie Wain was awarded the second VC. While seriously wounded, he left the safety of his tank to storm a German strong-point and take half its garrison prisoner, near Marcoing in the Hindenburg Support Line on 20 November 1917. Lieutenant Cecil Howard Sewell of the 3rd Battalion won the third VC for saving the life of other wounded, while injured himself, and giving his life in the process near Fremicourt on 29 April 1918. His light Whippet tank, named Caesar, is now in the Tank Museum. Lieutenant-Colonel Richard Annersley West received the fourth VC, also posthumously, for the double actions of Courcelles on 21 August and Vaulx-Vracourt on 2 September 1918 where he rallied his men in the face of certain death from machine-gun fire.

At home the coach company that was later known as Shamrock & Rambler, provided the Army with a charabanc – Rambler No. 4 carrying registration number EL 1250 – for a shuttle service between Lulworth and Bournemouth, with stops at Wareham and Poole en route. For an afternoon and evening out 'the return fare to Town was two shillings which

was docked from our pay.' Departure, from the Guard Room beside the west gate at Lulworth Camp, was at 2p.m. The return, from The Square at Bournemouth, was at 11p.m., passing through Poole at midnight.

After the First World War, hundreds of tanks accumulated in the Tank Park between Bovington Camp and Clouds Hill. A decade passed before they were broken up. But the tank could not be disinvented; new models were being designed and tested and a leaner peacetime Army was being trained. Forward thinkers warned that the next war might be unlike the previous one, moving on from static defences to armoured mobility. Consequently, the reluctant and reactionary War Office allowed the Tank Corps the cachet of Royal Tank Corps.

Bovington was used for mechanical and engineering training while gunnery was concentrated at Lulworth. The administrative headquarters was also at Bovington and as the camp at Lulworth expanded, children were taken by bus to Bovington School. There was resistance to permanent facilities being provided at Lulworth. In 1923 the War Department tired of its short lease and applied to purchase the Bindon Range. The first counter-attack was launched by the *Daily Mail*:

The assault on Lulworth Cove is of all those vandalistic enterprises the most inexcusable. The intention is to establish a Tank Gunnery School there. The Daily Mail *has always supported the cause of the tank against the 'bow and arrow' school at the War Office but we feel it is really preposterous to tell the British public that the only range suited for tanks is the most exquisitely beautiful stretch of the Wessex coast.*

A little investigation would prove that alternative sites can be found without any difficulty. If the War Office does not show itself reasonable the House of Commons will have to intervene to save the threatened area from its assailants.

Lulworth found a Dorset journalist to put the scenic case. Stuart Petre Brodie Mais (1885–1975), essayist and master at Sherborne School, pointed out that this stretch of coast was known as the 'English Bay of Naples'. He also seems to have been the first to make the pun about 'collecting shells on a Dorset beach.' Referring to a different kind of seashell he claimed, 'it is not a game that I recommend to the many Boy Scouts and Girl Guides who are in camp nearby.' The *Daily Graphic* printed his report:

Lulworth Cove itself was originally included in the scheme. So little do the authorities know of the country that when it was pointed out to them that their western boundary extended to a point 900 feet west of a beauty spot at least as famous and often visited as Clovelly they said 'west' was a misprint for 'east'.

Judged from the point of view of fair play, it is questionable morality to hire by force a plot of ground which was already prospected as an eligible site for a seaside resort, turn it into a wilderness, and then offer to buy it at wilderness rates. Not only is the area covered by the tanks turned from an artists' paradise into a scapegoats' hell, but the actual property of Lulworth Castle becomes valueless. They could not hit upon a worse plot of ground from every point of view. More and more it is becoming difficult for the townsman in search of a holiday to find some place that is both beautiful and quiet. The stretch of coast between Swanage and Lulworth is absolutely unspoilt.

No one is going to take a holiday in country where his way is constantly being barred owing to gun practice. Even now sentries demand passes before you are allowed over Bindon Hill. The danger area, by an amazing lack of foresight, includes the only Fossil Forest in Britain. Geologists and their pupils swarmed there. Now they will not be allowed to see it.

The fishermen of Lulworth depend largely for a living on their lobster pots: if they go in an easterly direction they have to be back before nine in the morning. They can no longer shelter in Mupe's Bay [Mupe Bay on the map but all the old fishermen called it Mupes] when they are unable to make Lulworth.

One of the fishermen told Mais, 'I fought for this bit of land and when I come home they try to starve me out of it.' The issue was put in even stronger terms by landowner Charles Joseph Weld-Blundell of Lulworth Castle, when he stated: '... even the Huns never did a thing like this!'

The *Bournemouth Daily Echo* reported on 30 November 1923 that not only was the future of the tank ranges under consideration but the War Office was considering the offer of an alternative site on the western side of the cove, towards White Nothe:

Up to the present the War Office has made no announcements to relieve public suspense regarding its intentions for the future of Lulworth Cove. At this week's meeting of the Dorset County Council it was reported that no reply had been received to the protest of the council against the proposal to establish the Tank Gunnery

The scene at the centre of Mupe Bay, looking eastwards over Mupe Rocks in a relatively lively sea, to Cockpit Head (left) and Worbarrow Bay. This stretch of coastline became out of bounds to tourists and fishermen alike once the area was absorbed by the Army for firing practice.

School permanently at East Lulworth, and the only information available for the county authority was a statement that it is possible the Army Council will not press the question of purchase of the site but will continue to lease it.

Lord Shaftesbury, the Lord Lieutenant of the county, could go further than that, and the County Council, equally with those people all over the country who wish to see our beauty spots preserved, must possess themselves in patience until the War Office thinks proper to give some indication of its attitude.

The principal reason advanced for suggesting that the War Office may not purchase the site was, in the opinion of experts in the tank arm of the service, that the obvious line of development of the tank is in the direction of heavier armament and that with heavier guns being used the Lulworth range might prove inadequate. There is another point that is always worth bearing in mind – that the War Office has an alternative site offered them on the west side of the cove which would not interfere with the famous beauty spot.

Weld-Blundell, Lulworth's owner, was joined by novelist Thomas Hardy and the Lord Lieutenant, as well as Lord Shaftesbury and West Lulworth resident Sir Alfred Fripp, in the struggle against permanent acquisition of 973 acres of land. This was situated between Little Bindon and Arish Mell but the public inquiry in 1924 faced lengthy arguments about just what had been proposed.

The War Office insisted there had merely been a clerical error in fixing the western boundary, caused by the insertion of the word 'west' instead of 'east', and made a statement to this effect. Because of the mistake it had been 'incorrectly assumed' by the press and public that Lulworth Cove itself had been intended for inclusion. The boundary, the statement continued, should have been specified as running to the east of the cove so that the range included Bindon Hill. Firing would be infrequent and would consist mainly of light machine-gun fire so that:

... as little inconvenience as possible would be caused to the public, the footpaths being allowed to be used on bank holidays, Saturday, Sundays and special occasions and that suitable approved by-laws would be drawn up.

135

These assurances were sufficient to defuse opposition. Objections were withdrawn. Weld-Blundell also compromised over the proposed acquisition. Rather than resist the Government and risk losing the freehold, he agreed to a long-term lease of Lulworth Camp and Bindon Range which remains the situation at the start of the twenty-first century. Expansion into the Heath Range and Tyneham Range in 1943 was followed in 1952 by purchase of the freehold but this did not affect the Lulworth arrangements. A strange coincidence is that a similar offering of improved public access deflated the Tyneham campaign which raged for a decade from 1967 to 1976. Whitehall simply pulled out the appropriate contingency plan for dealing with this sort of popular pressure.

Ironically, the first permanent buildings at both Bovington Camp and Lulworth Camp were built by enemy labour. The Lulworth buildings, eight houses at The Oval, stand close to the road junction opposite Burngate Farm at the north-east corner of the military compound. They were built by German prisoners of war in 1919. These men were held in a camp nearby and expressed relief to be working locally, having previously been marched to Wool and Bovington and back each day. That was a return journey of 12 miles. There they built a railway spur, a bridge across the River Frome, and the factory-sized Central Workshops in Bovington Camp. The camp mushroomed at a time when its most famous recruit – masquerading as Private Shaw – was Colonel Thomas Edward Lawrence (aka Lawrence of Arabia).

In 1924 the poet Rudyard Kipling visited Bovington and complained that no one appreciated the historical significance of the abandoned tanks. As a result, in 1925, two were put in a shed. They were Little Willie, the world's first tank, and Mother, the first fighting version. Each weighed 28 tons. Others soon joined them, forming the nucleus of the Tank Museum, although the Second World War exacted its toll on the exhibits.

Amanullah Khan, Amir of Afghanistan, visited Lulworth Camp on 20 March 1928. He was given a royal guard of honour at a time when he was accomplishing a delicate balancing act between two great powers. He attempted to maintain his country's independence by signing separate treaties with Great

Below: German prisoners of war from Lulworth marched to Wool, to build a branch railway line to Bovington Camp, where they constructed workshops.

Above: The Amir of Afghanistan, Amanullah Khan, who made treaties with both Britain and Soviet Russia, taking the salute at Lulworth on 20 March 1928.

Left: King George V, wearing a Royal Tank Corps beret (left), visiting the huts of Lulworth Camp in April 1928.

Tank Targets

Tank targets set in the slope of Whiteway Hill, looking towards scrubland near East Lulworth and Povington Heath beyond.

Britain and Soviet Russia. Both had – and would – mount Afghan expeditions. King George V followed in the Amir's Lulworth footsteps, receiving the same honour guard, in April 1928. As villagers were not allowed into the camp, through 'security or bloody-mindedness', Doug O'Hare recalls, they gathered together on the corner opposite Burngate Farmhouse:

Some official announced that the King and Queen were about to arrive, when who should appear but old man Chaffey in his brown Austin Seven. He was a smallish dumpy man with a beard. Needless to say all the crowd started cheering like mad. The King and Queen Mary arrived much later, by which time most of the crowd had got fed-up of waiting and gone home.

Captain Edward Body arrived at Lulworth Camp in 1929, before the building of its 'Tin Tabernacle', and recalled Sunday church parades. The Catholics had it easy, joining the Welds in the Castle grounds, but Anglicans were marched down Camp Hill and through West Lulworth with a band playing. They were continually admonished for their return performance, as a 'hobbling havoc' up the slope, to a tuneless rendition of My Boy Willie. In their midst strode the Commanding Officer, Lieutenant-Colonel Michael Denman Gambier-Parry (1891–1976), 'pushing the band and pulling the troops.'

By 1931 there were 515 men and their families living at Lulworth Camp. The legendary Lulworth figure, 'twice life-size', was Regimental Sergeant Major 'Snags' Hambley. His nickname came as a result of his catchphrase. 'Any snags, my boy?' he would ask whenever anyone hesitated. He could rise to any occasion, including quietly taking on and defusing the situation when the best boxer in the Tank Corps, much the worse for 'liquid engineering', was making himself a nuisance in Tin Shed Mess. He had refused to leave and then sat down to join a card game. Hambley went over to the table. 'May I?' he said, as if to shuffle the cards. Calmly, he proceeded to tear them in half, one by one, and said, 'Last show, tonight, gentlemen.' That was all it needed; the Mess emptied.

Catering at Lulworth became renowned after the arrival of a chef, fresh from the Captain's table on one of Cunard's Atlantic liners. He arrived in 1932, to feed the sergeants in Tin Shed Mess, and was soon head-hunted for the Officers' Mess where he stayed until 1949. With Charlie Whitlock's skills, and the availability of weapons and land, 1930s-style cordon bleu catering kept up standards all through wartime rationing, with rabbit as a constant stand-by if hare, pheasant and venison were off. Illicit supplies of shellfish came from the military seaboard. Sauces and curries made for an incredibly varied menu that was half a century ahead of its time.

Stage three of the expansion of the Lulworth Ranges was carried out in 1939 when the realities of a new war removed the necessity for the niceties of

Simulated gunnery practice at Lulworth Camp in 1940, with the backdrop to the tank turret being an authentic canvas of pines and telegraph poles beside the road across the heath from Holme Bridge to East Lulworth.

Halcombe Vale, in the foothills of Flower's Barrow, looking north-eastwards in the 1930s when Arish Mell was known for having cattle on the beach.

Obsolete tank used as a pillbox for machine-gunners, placed between Dragon's Teeth anti-tank obstacles in the Arish Mell Gap, when German invasion threatened in the summer of 1940.

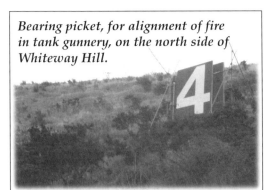

Bearing picket, for alignment of fire in tank gunnery, on the north side of Whiteway Hill.

Gate guard – a Centurion Mark XII – beside the entrance to the Armoured Fighting Vehicles Gunnery School at Lulworth Camp, pointing north-west in 2002.

Above: *Instructor at the Armoured Fighting Vehicles School, Lulworth Camp, showing how to clear stoppages on a Besa machine-gun in 1941.*

public consultation. Range by-laws were amended to include a larger danger area. The public was excluded and public paths, although they still existed as highways, were no longer usable even if the red danger flags had been lowered. A subtle change in the eastern boundary of Bindon Range, from the west to the east side of Arish Mell, took in a charming little bay that had been popular with picnickers and courting couples throughout the 1930s. 'There was always a cow on that beach,' my father told me, and produced an old snapshot to prove it.

Dragon's Teeth tank-traps were constructed and reinforced with obsolete tanks, including those from the Tank Museum, as stationary pillboxes for machine-gunners. Lulworth Camp and its Bindon Range were defended with 40mm Bofors anti-aircraft guns, as the Dorset coast found itself on the front line for the Battle of Britain after German forces streamed across northern France. The Luftwaffe's newly acquired bases on the Cherbourg peninsula allowed almost daily incursions across the Channel. Air raid warnings were commonplace but the unannounced lone German aircraft was potentially more dangerous.

One such opportunist sneaked toward Lulworth Camp just minutes after the siren sounded All Clear on 23 August 1940. 'Recruits had resumed their infantry training and were in the open as the aircraft approached,' to quote the diary entry in *Wartime Dorset:*

Sergeant J. Thompson shouted to them to get down and stay still. Eight bombs were dropped on the sports field, the ranges and St Andrew's Farm. Two men were killed and seven injured, the latter including Sergeant Thompson who received severe leg wounds. He had been in the stores when he heard the aircraft approaching and but for his instant and brave response, when he put himself in the line of fire to warn the men, there would have been a greater number of casualties.

The Gunnery Wing of the Armoured Fighting Vehicles School at Lulworth Camp rose to the occasion with makeshift solutions; it mounted Besa machine-guns in the turret of a light tank, to produce mobile batteries of anti-aircraft guns. Often airborne attackers were seen off by Spitfires from Warmwell Aerodrome, the Fighter Command station midway between Lulworth and Dorchester, and Hurricanes from RAF Exeter. They put down a number of enemy fighters and bombers, including the first Germans to be taken prisoner in the Battle of Britain, who crash-landed on Povington Heath, Tyneham, on 11 July 1940. Their Messerschmitt Bf.110, accompanied by 'Stuka' dive-bombers had been attacking Channel shipping but the majority of those intercepted were bombers and their escorts returning from raids on Bristol and other inland targets. Most of the enemy losses ended up in the sea.

There were also occasional British crashes. Sergeant Pilot Ernest Snowden of 213 Squadron lived to fight another day, on 11 August 1940, when he brought his crippled Hurricane down on C-Range at Lulworth. He had been hit by return fire as he shot down a Messerschmitt Bf.110.

Jubilant anti-aircraft gunners at Lulworth Camp brought down a Messerschmitt Bf.110 fighter-bomber on 27 September 1940. It crashed about 1,000 metres from the cliffs. The aircraft had been taking part in an abortive raid on the Parnall Aircraft Company at Yate, near Chipping Sodbury. Another Bf.110, which it appears belonged to Zerstorergeschwader 26, was involved in an attack on the Westland Aircraft factory at Yeovil in Somerset. In this attack, 100 civilians were killed in a direct hit on an air-raid shelter on 7 October 1940. The enemy plane later crashed into the sea, just 2,000 metres off the Arish Mell Gap and was claimed by Spitfires of 609 Squadron from Warmwell.

In July 1941 the Infantry Brigade of the Third Division, commanded by General Bernard Montgomery, arrived at Lulworth Camp from Abbotsbury. There veterans of the Dunkirk beaches had been chosen for conversion to armour. They were equipped with the new Churchill tank, after training at Lulworth and Bovington, and sailed with Montgomery to war in the Western Desert. There, with the Eighth Army, the famous victory took place over Rommel's Afrika Korps at El Alamein.

The increased movements of tanks, of growing weight, between Bovington and Lulworth via Wool, led to the Christchurch-based bridging unit of the Military Engineering Experimental Establishment, being asked to provide one of its first Bailey Bridges in the summer of 1941. This was put in place across the River Frome, eastwards and midway to Wareham, beside the narrow and historic Holme Bridge at East Stoke. The Meccano-like solution, after being used by the Allies in operations across the globe, won a knighthood for Donald Coleman Bailey of Viking Close at Southbourne. Military movements between Bovington and Lulworth, even at the beginning of the new millennium, still involve traversing the new Holme Bridge.

Spitfire R6639 of 53 Operational Training Unit made a crash landing at West Lulworth whilst attempting a forced landing on 10 September 1941. The following month, on 21 October, there was a huge explosion beside Lulworth Cove when a Focke-Wulf 190 flew in low from the sea and crashed into the side of Bindon Hill. As the plane was not shot down, it was assumed that the German pilot had misjudged his position and course.

On 6 April 1942, Lulworth Camp entertained the Prime Minister who came as the war-lord 'to see my tanks.' These were the British-made machines that bore his name. He inspected them from the side of Halcombe Vale, above Sea Vale Farm, in sight of Arish Mell. To quote once again from *Wartime Dorset*:

War Premier Winston Churchill inspecting the new tanks bearing his name, at Halcombe Vale above Sea Vale Farm, with accompanying top-brass on 6 April 1942.

Recruitment poster for the Royal Armoured Corps on the Lulworth Ranges – 'would you like to crew one of these vehicles?'

Ranks of Churchill tanks, the first to go into service, received their namesake's approval today in the Arish Mell valley on the Dorset coast. Prime Minister Winston Churchill had a full tour of the Gunnery Wing of the Armoured Fighting Vehicles School at Lulworth Camp. Some of the Churchill tanks have been refitted with 6-pounder guns to give them much increased fire-power. The first production versions carry 2-pounders.

Tanks & The Second World War

Below: *Cruiser tanks on the Bindon Range, lining up for firing practice towards Bindon Hill, in a view looking north-west towards woodland around Lulworth Park, 1941.*

Valentine light tank, mounting a 6-pounder anti-tank gun, at Lulworth Camp in 1942.

Right: *Quad Besa machine-guns mounted as a mobile anti-aircraft battery in 1941 and used in the defence of Lulworth Camp.*

Below: *General Grant, a newly introduced American tank, being put through its paces at Lulworth Camp in April 1942.*

Above: *Specimen Panzers, captured from the Wehrmacht in the Battle of Normandy, were brought to Lulworth for evaluation and test-firings on the tank gunnery ranges.*

The workshop at Lulworth Camp was strafed on 14 December 1942. This left it in 'an utter shambles', with Sergeant Jack Stevens fatally wounded and three other soldiers injured. Two German fighter-bombers had carried out a surprise attack, approaching from the east across the Tank Park, and then turned south-west to disappear over Lulworth Cove and out to sea.

The war moved from the defensive years and into the offensive end-game. The whole of Dorset was being turned into a military camp, for 80,000 Americans, when the War Cabinet gave the secret order for the evacuation of the whole of Tyneham parish and adjoining areas inland to East Holme. This fourth and final extension of the Lulworth Ranges, expanding it to 7,500 acres, took place six days before Christmas in 1943 and was principally done for the training of Sherman tank crews of the Second Armored Division of the First United States Army. They were tasked for the Battle of Normandy and sailed for France in support of the infantry of V Corps, after beach-head O for Omaha had been secured in the D-Day landings.

The Luftwaffe threat diminished as the Germans retreated eastwards but E-boat incursions, by high-speed German gunboats, mines and submarines continued to take their toll on Allied shipping. *Black Hawk*, a crippled United States

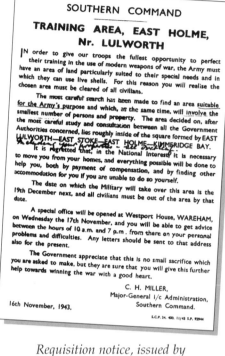

SOUTHERN COMMAND

TRAINING AREA, EAST HOLME, Nr. LULWORTH

IN order to give our troops the fullest opportunity to perfect their training in the use of modern weapons of war, the Army must have an area of land particularly suited to their special needs and in which they can use live shells. For this reason you will realise the chosen area must be cleared of all civilians.

The most careful search has been made to find an area suitable for the Army's purpose and which, as the same time, will involve the smallest number of persons and property. The area decided on, after the most careful study and consultation between all the Government Authorities concerned, lies roughly inside of the square formed by EAST LULWORTH—EAST STOKE—EAST HOLME—KIMMERIDGE BAY.

It is regretted that, in the National Interest it is necessary to move you from your homes, and everything possible will be done to help you, both by payment of compensation, and by finding other accommodation for you if you are unable to do so yourself.

The date on which the Military will take over this area is the 19th December next, and all civilians must be out of the area by that date.

A special office will be opened at Westport House, WAREHAM, on Wednesday the 17th November, and you will be able to get advice between the hours of 10 a.m. and 7 p.m. from there on your personal problems and difficulties. Any letters should be sent to that address also for the present.

The Government appreciate that this is no small sacrifice which you are asked to make, but they are sure that you will give this further help towards winning the war with a good heart.

C. H. MILLER,
Major-General i/c Administration,
Southern Command.

16th November, 1943.

S.C.P. 24. 400. 11/43 S.P. 92944

Requisition notice, issued by Major-General Charles Harvey Miller on 16 November 1943, for a massive expansion of what became the Lulworth and East Holme Ranges.

steam-freighter, was brought into Worbarrow Bay on 29 December 1944. Her stern had been blown to pieces by a torpedo from a U-boat, but the crew were able to scramble to safety after beaching her bows.

As the Allied tanks rolled across France they captured specimens of enemy armoured vehicles, which were sent back to Lulworth for evaluation and firing trials. These showed the advanced technology and fire-power of German machines, better than those of the Allies in all but numbers, and lacking vital aerial protection. Some are preserved in the Tank Museum. The museum's revival came about in 1947 when there was renewed interest in the discarded tanks rusting around Lulworth. Those vintage specimens that had not been scrapped were gathered up again from the heaths and coast and put back into the museum. Little Willie had survived. So too had examples of Mark I, IV, V, VIII and IX. There was also a miniature British tank, the 14-ton Whippet, from 1916, and a Peerless armoured car built in 1917.

The Government decided in 1948 to retain Tyneham parish, despite acknowledging that promises had been given that it would be returned. The onset of the Cold War had made this decision irreversible.

As the main British battle-tank evolved from Churchill, Cromwell and Crusader to Centurion,

A gas bomb dropped by a Lysander biplane on a Sherman tank in an exercise near East Lulworth in 1943, looking south-east to an instantly recognisable backdrop of the Purbeck Hills, between Povington Hill and Whiteway Hill.

Chieftain and Conqueror, veterans recalled their Lulworth days. The comedian Arthur English, who rose to fame as the 'Wide Boy' and became known to wireless listeners across the globe through the Variety Bandbox programme, was an instructor in the Gunnery Wing of the Armoured Fighting Vehicles School. 'It's nice to think that the boys at Lulworth still remember me,' he told *The Tank* magazine. He continued:

A lot of water's passed under the bridge since I was there – some of it pretty chilly. But I don't have to run to Wool to catch the Passion Wagon to Bournemouth any more, and it seems a long time since I had a pint at the Castle.

I had a rough time when I came out of the Army. I was navvying on the roads for six months until I got a job as a painter at Aldershot, but all the time I was trying to get a break into show business. My chance didn't come until I got an audition at the Windmill and Mr Vivian van Damm (Officer Commanding, Windmill Girls) gave me a job on the spot. I've been resident comedian there ever since and I can tell you that the faces you see in the Windmill canteen are a lot easier on the eye than some of those I remember in the Sergeants' Mess at Lulworth.

In the 1930s the movies were a bus journey away, in Bill Bugg's Garrison Theatre at Bovington Camp, but Lulworth came into its own during the Second World War. Its speciality were the ENSA shows, performed by the Entertainments National Service Association – which had its acronym parodied as Every Night Something Awful. These shows often featured fast-moving humour. Here are a couple of jokes that made the transition from camp to village and might just bear repetition:

Male: *I've got this medical condition which means that every time I sneeze I have an uncontrollable urge to grab the nearest woman.*
Female: *What are you doing about it?*
Male: *Taking snuff!*

Female: *Be serious. I know you have lots of lady admirers. What's the secret behind a perfect kiss?*
Male artist: *Siphoning petrol!*

Married quarters for soldiers were provided beside Lulworth Camp with 18 houses being built in Vale Road in 1952. Another 13 were for officers, around the corner in Bindon Close, with sea views across Weymouth Bay to Portland. Many of the wartime huts on the camp were demolished in 1954 and replacement facilities included a new cookhouse and dining room. A new moving target was built on the Heath Range. Called 'Movers' these lengths of rail, protected by a bank, enabled much more challenging and realistic training than having tank crews merely firing at static positions. Those on Bindon Range were out of action in 1959 while digging took place for the outfall pipe from the Atomic Energy Establishment at Winfrith, down Sea Vale and into the sea, through the Arish Mell Gap.

New-generation warfare became standard at Lulworth in 1960. Having cancelled Orange William, an anti-tank missile developed by Fairey Aviation, the War Office looked to the other side of the globe and ordered 400 Malkara surface-to-surface weapons. These 222-pound wire-guided anti-tank missiles, designed and manufactured by Australia's nationalised aircraft industry, were mounted in pairs on Humber Hornet scout cars that had been converted into rocket launchers.

Firing tests were carried out in Tyneham valley where the trees and scrub became draped with discarded wire. What was originally intended as an anti-tank weapon, with a 57-pound warhead, was found to perform equally well against static targets such as bridges and blockhouses. 'Its accuracy is such that it can be guided through the openings in a concrete bunker or gun emplacement from more than a mile away,' it was reported.

Malkara and its air-droppable Hornet armoured fighting vehicles became standard equipment for the British Army. Cyclops Squadron of the 2nd Royal Tank Regiment was fitted out with Hornet-Malkara combinations as a 'go anywhere' unit that could be airlifted by Argosy and other RAF transport planes.

Over the years I have researched a bizarre and at the time top-secret aircraft crash which took place 40 miles south of Lulworth Cove, at 6.55a.m. Central European Time, on Friday 23 May 1969. Sergeant Paul Adams Meyer and a stolen Lockheed C130E Hercules – a 30-ton military turbo-prop carrying advanced electronics – exploded in mid-Channel at co-ordinates 50.00 N (latitude), 02.05 W (longitude). Aircraft serial number 37789 belonging to the 513th Tactical Air Wing of the 3rd Air Force USAFE (United States Air Force, Europe) had gone missing from the big air base at Mildenhall in East Anglia.

Meyer, who had emotional problems and had been drinking heavily, was an Assistant Crew Chief on the ground. Despite being 'restricted to barracks' and grounded he stole the keys of a vehicle, reached Hercules 37789 on hardstand 21, assumed the name Captain Epstein, and had it loaded with 60,000 gallons of fuel. He 'taxied from the hardstand' at 5.06a.m. Central European Time on Thursday 22 May and began his unauthorised 'take-off roll' as vehicles weaved across the runway and tried to stop him.

Paul Meyer had enough fuel for a flight of 5,000 miles. The initially 'erratic flight path' was replaced by automatic navigation and he headed towards the Atlantic and phoned his wife in Virginia. She talked him into turning back and landing at a British airfield. The rest of the story is contained in the USAF Accident/Incident Report,

Tyneham

Left: *The evacuation of picturesque Tyneham village, and all 3,003 acres of the next parish east of Lulworth, took place on 19 December 1943.*

Below: *John Gould and his message that nearly succeeded in releasing the Lulworth Ranges. Photographed near the ruins of his home by Rodney Legg in 1973.*

Above: *Deputation to call for the release of the Lulworth Ranges with campaigners Mavis Caver and Rodney Legg entering No. 10 Downing Street in 1973.*

John Gould was born at TYNEHAM 60 YEARS AGO HE WANTS TO COME HOME

Left: *Christmas wreath for Prime Minister Harold Wilson, held by Tyneham-born John Gould, marking the 30th anniversary of the occupation of his village, accompanied by Mavis Caver, Philip Watkins and Lord Fenner Brockway.*

Above: *Final wreath of the campaign, placed by Rodney Legg in Tyneham Parish Church on 19 December 1993, to mark the 50th anniversary of the eviction of the villagers.*

but the version released through the United States Freedom of Information Act has crucial words, sentences and paragraphs censored with a black marker. Some have been removed for personal reasons but other details have been removed because the information is considered to be classified. It is questionable as to what extent the aircraft was visible or invisible on radar screens – it allegedly had stealth capabilities – and just how it met its end. One theory is that Meyer was talked into activating a 'destructor' button to prevent him bringing it back over land. Another account, suggesting he was on course for Russia, says the Hercules was shot down. The official explanation from Mildenhall was that Meyer had tried to ditch in the sea; wreckage was found in the Channel:

It takes a highly trained and skilled pilot to land on the sea. There's a strong possibility the plane broke up... Sergeant Meyer is still missing and presumed dead of injuries sustained when the aircraft hit the water.

On land, the cause célèbre to release the Lulworth Ranges picked up momentum in 1969, fuelled by emotional calls by the last of those born at Tyneham 'to honour Churchill's pledge' and let them return home, to a backdrop of press and television pictures of ruined cottages. Clay-mining was allowed to continue on the heath but no one could return. 'Surrender Purbeck' slogans painted on Army signs, and trespassing for a candlelit carol service in the depopulated village on the anniversary of its occupation, were followed by persistent political action in London. Tyneham Action Group and its successor 1943 Committee instigated a House of Lords debate, delivery of a wreath to Harold Wilson at 10 Downing Street, and deputations to his Army Minister, Lord Brayley, and to Lord Carrington when he was Secretary of State for Defence.

Creation along the Lulworth coast of the South West Peninsula Coast Path, as part of England's longest long-distance footpath in 1973, brought the spectacular scenery to the fore with calls for 'bridging the gap between Lulworth and Kimmeridge.' This gave civil servants an idea for defusing the campaign with a classic British compromise. Although initially regarded by the military as 'unthinkable' on live-fire gunnery ranges, it was eventually decided that public access should be granted to the Lulworth Ranges on a scale that was unprecedented.

General Sir Roy Redgrave, writing his *Balkan Blue* memoirs in 2000, looked back to 1975 when he was Commandant of the Royal Armoured Corps Centre at Bovington and Lulworth. He quotes me as the critic who gave him full credit for what he describes as his 'second lasting achievement.' The first had been to sell the wine-lake held by the Officers' Mess at Bovington in order to fund a swimming pool, which was unauthorised but was filled with water when it was admired by Field-Marshal Sir Michael Carver, Chief of the Defence Staff. He 'came to unveil a portrait of himself in the Mess'. From that moment all was well except that the Mess Secretary who built up the precious wine cellar died at the end of a dinner that had been held in his honour. The next piece of applied diplomacy was more complicated:

I was told to form a working party to decide the best way to complete a missing link in the West Country coastal path which runs for 510 miles. This meant opening up the area between Lulworth Cove and Kimmeridge Bay and giving access to Tyneham village and Worbarrow Bay. The area was and still is of exceptional interest to ecologists, botanists and naturalists, but there was also the constant problem of dangerous unexploded shells.

I let it be known in the press what I was trying to achieve and was taken aback by the number of different groups, all with conflicting interests, who insisted on having a say in our decisions. I refused to have a public meeting but agreed to meet every single one of them individually and listen to their ideas. It was soon apparent that they nearly all had tunnel vision focused solely on their own aims to the exclusion of anybody else's needs.

For instance one group wanted the path to follow the exact line of the cliff tops, but the bird watchers said this would upset sea birds nesting below. Geologists wanted the Fossil Forest avoided, archaeologists wanted the paths to avoid the Iron-Age hill-fort, others wanted there to be access for caravans and tents and so on. But there was always something they said which I felt sure we could incorporate, whilst the other ideas we would consider. I promised to let them have early copies of our minutes and decisions, and if there was no comment received within 48 hours, we would go ahead. This formula worked well and with the necessary help from the Government to pay wardens, with no camping or fires allowed, no stalls allowed to sell anything, no motorcycles or horses on the paths, we opened a route across one of Dorset's most beautiful areas, which had been left totally unspoilt by farmers and modern developers. I was delighted when a magazine editor, Rodney Legg, who had been a constant critic of the Army, was generous enough to say in his editorial under the heading 'In Redgrave Park':

"The virtual conversion of a major Army range from a weekday training ground into a weekend public park has been masterminded by Brigadier Redgrave. He has coped successfully with balancing traditional military activities and new mass access plans. Redgrave, who deserves Public Relations Officer of the Year award for his achievement leaves Bovington in November."

And so it was to be. All good things had to come to an end but I was taken completely by surprise to be told that my next posting was to be to that stimulating and exciting city, Berlin.

New Generation Warfare

*Swingfire anti-tank missile, which became operational with the British Army in 1969,
on trials at Lulworth.*

*The Australian developed Malkara wire-guided anti-tank missile, fired from a Hornet armoured car,
was tested at Lulworth and Tyneham from 1966.*

New Generation Warfare

Ancient burial mound at Thorn Barrow, Povington, re-shaped by tank tracks and Army concrete, 1971.

The moving target extending from Thorn Barrow (right) looking north-eastwards across Povington Heath to Botany Wood.

Left: *Miscellaneous armour on the hard-standing east of Lulworth Camp, in a view northwards from Bindon Hill in 1981.*

Right: *A troop of Scorpions advance towards Maiden Plantation and targets in the Arish Mell Gap, as part of a firepower demonstration. A light field gun is in the foreground.*

Left: *Armour rolls along Purbeck's inland boundary, beside Five Barrow Hill on Povington Heath, in a panorama south-westwards to the woods of East Lulworth. Photographed by Colin Graham in 1985.*

Architecture at Lulworth Camp has evolved fitfully. The lines of huts that were built in the First World War continued to be used throughout changing times and designations; the Gunnery Wing of the Armoured Fighting Vehicles School became the Tactical School, alongside brick-built high-storey and multiple-wing buildings of the 1930s. Almost incongruously, and displacing 65-year-old huts, the space-age lines of the Maintenance Hangars arose in 1989, to shelter A-Vehicle complex.

The winter of 1990/1, following the Iraqi invasion of Kuwait, was a busy time for Lulworth as Challenger battle tanks were shipped from Germany and Britain for the two weeks of ground warfare that took place in the Gulf War. Operation Granby turned into Operation Desert Storm. The 1st Armoured Division led by Lieutenant-General Sir Peter de la Billiere, comprising the 4th and 7th Armoured Brigades and supported by a total of 35,000 British troops, was one of the key elements of Coalition VII Corps, under the central command of American General Norman Schwarzkopf.

The Royal Fleet Auxiliary Logistics Landing Ship L3004, *Sir Bedivere*, was active in the Gulf between 10 October 1990 and 11 April 1991. She brought home Scorpions of the 2nd Royal Tank Regiment, which were delivered to the Ranges at Lulworth as part of an amphibious landing in Worbarrow Bay.

When the Cold War was won without a shot having been fired, the Lulworth Ranges saw the destruction of 183 earlier 'over-quota' Chieftain tanks. They were later blown up, as targets in 1993–4, in front of Russian observers. Colonel Sergei Slepnev witnessed their end: 'Two years ago I would never have thought this day possible but it is to be welcomed and I have been impressed by what I have seen here in Britain.'

Challenger tank at Bindon View Point, on the north-east side of Lulworth Camp, in a 1997 shot by Rodney Legg looking south-east across long shadows to the entrenchments of Flower's Barrow hill-fort, etched on the skyline.

Roadside warning, near Burngate Farm, of what has been the Lulworth sound for nearly a century.

Warning sign for walkers to stay within the paths on the Lulworth Ranges, between marker posts.

Exploring the Ranges

Above: *Walking the Ranges, correctly placed between yellow-painted marker posts, in a climb northwards up Cockpit Head from Mupe Bay, in 1995.*

Right: *Familiar trespasser Rodney Legg inspecting a shell hole on the Lulworth Ranges, on Povington Heath, in 1971.*

Left: *Weekend welcome signs at Burngate Farm, with the Lulworth Range Walks open for business.*

Clay Extraction

Right: *Detail of the clay seam being worked beneath the crane, with the usual suspect for scale, photographed at Povington in 1972.*

Left: *Industrial archaeology from what is now a bygone age, with the head-gear of an underground clay mine, inside the Lulworth Ranges, at West Creech in 1972.*

Modern ball clay extraction from a great open pit below Povington Hill, which made headlines as 'the biggest hole in Dorset', photographed by Colin Graham, northwards across the Lulworth Ranges to Raymond's Firs (centre), in 1972.

Chapter 20

LANDSCAPE CAMEOS

Monica Hutchings, the author of doctor and nurse romances who came to live at Church Knowle where she wrote about Dorset and had a regular column in the *Western Gazette*, frequently reminded me of the historic boundaries defining the Isle of Purbeck. To the south, east and north there is no problem; going round the coast of the English Channel, and then from Swanage Bay to Studland Bay, the third side is Poole Harbour and its islands, all of which belong to Purbeck parishes.

Then comes the difficulty. On the western side the Isle of Purbeck, there is no island. It attaches to the landscape of south Dorset and most of us think of it extending along the chalk hills to include both East and West Lulworth. Monica insisted otherwise.

Sheep folded between hurdles to work their way across a field in the high uplands between West Lulworth, Coombe Keynes and Winfrith Newburgh in 1969.

Firstly, however, she would correct all comers that the short title of the Isle of Purbeck is simply 'Purbeck'. Never 'the Purbecks'. That was incorrect, anathema and taboo.

The second lost cause concerned the western boundary. The island ended at the western end of the Purbeck Hills at Flower's Barrow hillfort and this fourth side then ran inland to the little stream known as Luckford Lake and followed it northwards to the River Frome which is the fifth and final line, along its tidal length to the harbour at Swineham Point.

Luckford Lake is an overly impressive name for the only geographical feature on Purbeck's landward boundary that is worthy of being called a boundary. It is a marshy tributary of

Lulworth car park before the motor cars, in 1897. Looking south-eastwards over the Coastguard Cottages to beach huts on the far side of the cove and Little Bindon beyond.

the Frome, which it joins at Stoke Common in the parish of East Stoke. The southern end trickles from the sloping fields north of Lulworth Park and meanders across the heath beneath a canopy of sallow scrub.

The name 'Lake' is also less expansive than it sounds, deriving from the Old English 'lacu' for 'watercourse'. It runs for two kilometres as a reasonable stream before mingling unnoticed with a concourse of branches of the Frome at West Holme. Even its head is disputable as the stream forms from a collection of smaller waters that can be traced towards ruined Whiteway Farm, road drains in East Lulworth, and a trickle in Monkton Bushes near the site of sixteenth-century Woodstreet Farm which was demolished in the 1960s. The latter joins a ditch from Coombe Lots. The only impressive source is the overflow from The Lake, behind Home Farm, between East Lulworth and Coombe Keynes.

Here the countryside changes with the geology. The mixed soils are marked with a belt of woods, the names of which show how well popular etymology can describe the countryside – Long Coppice and Highwood (East Stoke parish); Monkton Bushes, Pepperclose Trees, Knap Coppice and Haremere Wood (Wool parish); Vicarage Coppice, Bramble Coppice, Eweyard Coppice, Kick

Hill Coppice, Vary Clump, Ashy Drove, Duckpond Plantation, Kennel Wood and Lake Hill Plantation (Coombe Keynes parish); Gore Holmes, Seven Acre Withy Bed, Lodgewood, New Barn Plantation, Bowling Green Wood, Botany Wood, Broom's Plantation, Marl Plantation and Maiden Plantation (East Lulworth parish).

No one, apart from Monica Hutchings, has taken Luckford Lake seriously and it is only partially used for parish boundaries. It is an arbitrary border for Purbeck and fails to cut a clear line from the hilly seaward chalk. John Leyland, Henry VIII's historian, confirms that Monica was right, as he claims, 'where as the limits of East Lulworth do end there beginneth Purbeck forest ground.' His use of the word 'forest' is in its ancient usage, as hunting territory, rather than to imply it is wooded. Thomas Gerard, writing his *Survey of Dorsetshire* in the 1620s, supplies more detail:

And now we come to the Island of Purbeck which surely is but a peninsula, for from this place, Lulworth, there is good passage into it without crossing any water at all. It lieth in length seven miles; in breadth not more than half as much. Bounded on the south and east with the

Above: *H.T. Simpson of Newlands Farm, who died in 1973.*

Left: *Cereal fields north of West Lulworth looking east to West Down Farm in 1995.*

Right: *Sheep country, in the Belhuish valley, looking north-eastwards in 1997.*

Barns at Belhuish Farm, in downland near old Lulworth Common. Frome Valley can be glimpsed looking north-west.

The flock of sheep that were grounded at Burngate Farm in West Lulworth, during the foot-and-mouth epidemic of 2001.

Background: *Scratchy Bottom, with Durdle Door beyond, was chosen by film-maker John Schlesinger for the opening scene in his Hardy classic,* **Far from the Madding Crowd.**

Top right: *Portland view, from Scratchy Bottom, where Gabriel Oak's sheep were driven over the cliff in the film of* Far from the Madding Crowd.
Bottom right: *The name on the landscape, with its path signed between fence and heifer.*

British Sea, on the north with the River Frome, which there falleth into a safe and large harbour called Poole; on the west with a moorish lake, which runneth into the Frome named Luckford Lake.

The real barriers of both nature and the mind are those that were set in the boundary changes of 1972 and came into legal effect on 1 April 1974 with the creation of Purbeck District Council. This covers 100,160 acres (156.5 square miles) of south-east Dorset. That doubled the size of Monica's Purbeck. It does, however, give a superb physical end-point to Purbeck's western seaboard, with the former Coastguard Cottages at 495 feet on White Nothe, which are the highest buildings on the Dorset coast. Their western garden wall marks the extremity of Chaldon Herring parish, which is the next beyond West Lulworth. All three Lulworth communities can now be regarded as within rather than without the Isle of Purbeck.

The coastal parishes are linked now by the South West Peninsula Coast Path, Britain's longest long-distance official footpath when it opened in 1974, which has its roots in the tracks used by coastguards until 1913, tramping at night between white-painted marker stones as Excisemen of the anti-smuggling Preventive Service. Sea Fencibles followed, as forerunners of the Home Guard, and current peacetime users of the route have made it the busiest of our long-haul

leisure paths. The section above Lulworth Cove, wide and white in exposed track, must be a candidate for the most intensely used rural public footpath in the land.

It leads to Durdle Door and the wonderfully named Scratchy Bottom where a dry valley ends in a precipice above the sea. This provided the opening setting for the renowned film of one of Thomas Hardy's best known novels. *Far from the Madding Crowd*, John Schlesinger's classic production of 1967, with music by Richard Rodney Bennett, opens with Alan Bates, as shepherd Gabriel Oak, on his farm. The scene comes back into the story when his over-enthusiastic sheepdog drives the flock along Scratchy Bottom from Newlands Warren and sheep fall onto the beach above the Bull Rock.

Lulworth returns to the story in both the book and the film, albeit two kilometres further west in the latter, when Terence Stamp as Sergeant Frank Troy did his disappearing act into the sea beside Durdle Door. His clothes are found on the beach and he is presumed to have drowned. Thomas Hardy was the first with the idea that our generation identifies with runaway Government minister John Stonehouse, in Miami, and Reggie Perrin, on the 'telly'. Some of Hardy's images are a little overblown. He called Portland the 'Gibraltar of Wessex' and also went way beyond reasonable exaggeration, on the same theme at Lulworth, by likening the two points beside the entrance to the cove to the 'Pillars of Hercules'.

Evocative symbols, in some cases, are recent additions to the landscape. The sculptor Peter Randall-Page carved fossil-period gastropods in Purbeck marble for dry-stone niches constructed by Charles Brentnall in the style of eastern wayside shrines. This was done as part of the 'New Milestones Project' commissioned by the community landscape charity, Common Ground, and the Weld estate in 1985. Randall-Page told me:

I have always thought Purbeck marble to be one of the most beautiful native stones we have in this country and I felt that the look of preciousness that this material has would enhance the sense of intimacy I wanted to achieve... In the event I found that Purbeck marble is no longer quarried and was extremely lucky to find a small number of pieces which had been quarried over 20 years ago.

He chose three cliff-top locations for the snail carvings, into a grassy bank immediately inland from the upper coastal path, across the downland between Durdle Door and White Nothe.

In the valley north-west of Burngate Farm lives Roderick Victor Miller. His middle name marks one of the milestone dates of the twentieth century. Rod Miller was born on 4 May 1945, the date Field-Marshal Sir Bernard Montgomery received the surrender on Luneberger Heide of German forces in northern Europe. He has since faced his own good fight in the Lulworth countryside for the future of his chosen craft, which keeps the roof on our time-warped corner of English countryside. As a thatcher he not only does the work but returns to the deep-cut Belhuish valley, below the former Lulworth Common, to argue his case against a combination of material shortages, interference from planners, and the strictures of Sir Jocelyn Stevens, one-time head of English Heritage.

Rod Miller's career has overlapped the sea change in England's traditional rural roofing:

I took up thatching because I was interested in this kind of work, even at school, and in 1966 the Weld estate was looking for a thatcher and I came from Wiltshire to take it up. In those days the estate had over 300 thatched properties; which is a lifetime's work. They still have a number at East and West Lulworth but most are sold off. We've now got five of us thatching, sub-contracting for me, and we go from Brittany to Shropshire, and across the Home Counties to East Anglia.

My three interviews with Rod Miller have spanned his three decades in the business. Its commercial side is managed by Pam Miller, his wife, and has expanded to import 200,000 bundles of reed a year from Poland, Hungary, Turkey and South Africa.

Left: *Thatcher Rod Miller with his stockpile of quality reed, behind Belhuish Farm.*

Right: *Cutting spars; a thatcher's winter work indoors.*

This has become necessary as changing farming methods in Britain and Europe have turned both wheat-straw and water-reed into scarce commodities. Rod explains:

They are our basic raw materials but what home-grown supply there is has become too expensive. There is more on offer but that is of unsuitable quality for lasting work. The older varieties of wheat that were traditionally used are no longer grown. In Dorset we've lost the reed beds at Radipole and Lodmoor, which are bird sanctuaries now, and also from Ridge and Arne in Purbeck. There we had 23 acres of reed. My brother, Ron Miller, had another 15 to 20 acres on the Wareham side of the water, on Swineham Point. Rodney Martin was reed-cutting in Lytchett Bay. All that was being harvested but now the only operational reed-bed in Dorset is at Abbotsbury. There used to be a five-shilling licence to cut reed on Radipole backwater, for use on hayricks, but no one thatches haystacks any more.

Rod Miller's long-running battle with English Heritage has been to counter their received wisdom that wheat rather than reed is the authentic thatching material in the western counties. In Dorset, he points out, not only were there great acreages of commercial reed-beds beside Poole Harbour and The Fleet lagoon but the mainstay of inland farming was dairying rather than grain fields. Furthermore, as he demonstrates with photographs of his own local roofs as proof, the dispute derives from a fallacy:

There is no difference in the style as such. A competent thatcher can make a water-reed roof look like a wheat-straw roof and my job is to give people the best possible roof at the most reasonable price. Longevity is the most important criterion. We now have councils offering small grants towards wheat-straw which in many cases only gives 10 or 15 years' life, even though it looks the same as water-reed thatching, which lasts twice as long. It's not just anecdote. There's hard evidence.

Rod Miller accuses conservation officers and the National Trust of searching for spurious short-term authenticity. He argues that the location and appearance of cottages should dictate the style of their thatching. In the exposed coastal zone of the Isle of Purbeck and across the heaths towards Dorchester and Poole the basic look would have been 'poor shallow-pitched roofs.' Specimen buildings, such as Woodsford Castle, would have received different treatment, and the general quality of buildings improved as one moved inland. Listed building regulations do owners no favours, as Rod explains:

Stripping old thatch has been barred but at some point it has to come off if the timbers have gone. They say you have to replace like with like but done well no one can tell the difference. I had to look up under the eaves of cottages at Burton Bradstock in order to say which was which – water-reed or wheat-straw – because they are identical when seen from the street.

The Miller family home, Belhuish Farmhouse, is at the end of a no through-road into the valley. The little lane that drops down from the main road is known as Old Hill. The farmhouse is substantially of seventeenth and eighteenth-century date with later additions. Walkers can explore further, with downland on the western slope having been part of the medieval Lulworth Common. It has lost its common grazing rights but grassland has been restored to something of its former floristic richness through a Countryside Stewardship scheme.

On the northern extremity of West Lulworth parish, south-facing slopes are out of the wind and alive with butterflies in summertime, including the natural history speciality that will round off our Lulworth story. It is the butterfly discovered in the parish and given its name. *Thymelicus acteon*, the diminutive Lulworth Skipper, was first drawn and described as a British species by John Curtis in March 1833. He described the specimen:

... discovered at Lulworth Cove in Dorsetshire, last August, by J.C. Dale Esq., through whose liberality it now ornaments most of our cabinets. It was found among thistles and was very local.

Dale, the High Sheriff of Dorset, was lucky in his choice of high summer for a trip to the seaside because the Lulworth Skipper is only on the wing for a period of about six weeks – from mid July to late August. As well as the purple flowers of the thistle they flit about around rest-harrow and marjoram. Dale's original first specimens are preserved with his collections at Oxford.

His son, Charles William Dale of Glanvilles Wootton, listed and described Dorset and British butterflies in 1889. He wrote that the 'exact place that the specimen was captured is called Durdle Door.' Or, rather, that is what he intended to write. It's the first time I've deliberately ended a book with what was known as a 'typo' in the days of hot-metal printing. Dale's typesetter stumbled over the handwriting and rendered 'Door' as 'Dove'.

The Lulworth Skipper now has its own conservation lobbyists based just a wing-beat away. The national environmental charity, Butterfly Conservation, moved its offices from Compton House, Sherborne, into the Manor Yard at East Lulworth. The official opening ceremony was carried out by television's *Ground Force* gardener, Alan Titchmarsh, on 27 September 2001. He planted a buddleia 'butterfly bush' to mark the occasion. He was welcomed by the society's chairman, Dr Stephen Jeffcoate, who also introduced Wilfrid Weld, representing the Weld estate, and Ian Knight MP.

Founded in 1968, Butterfly Conservation has grown into the world's foremost body for the promotion of 'insect rights'. It concentrates on the protection of habitat to ensure viable population numbers.

Above: *Television gardener Alan Titchmarsh opening the Butterfly Conservation offices at Lulworth in 2001, with Dr Stephen Jeffcoate and a delighted Linda Fear.*

Below: The environmental charity, Butterfly Conservation, has its new national home in the Manor Yard at East Lulworth.

*Hambury Tout, ascended by the chalky path – typical of the coast and countryside westwards from Lulworth
Cove with Portland on one horizon and caravans amid the pines towards Durdle Door (right).*

The plants, and the butterflies, moths and other insects feeding on them, form the basis of the entire natural foodchain. Scientific studies show how the process works and education is aimed at getting the message across.

Richard Fox explained that butterflies were vital indicators of the general health of the environment as could be seen, in the positive sense, on coastal downland above Lulworth Cove:

Only a few paces from the car park, on the steep track up Hambury Tout, weary hikers can watch for national rarities like the Adonis blue, with its brilliant sky-blue wings, shining in the sunlight, the camouflaged grayling, and our local speciality, the Lulworth Skipper.

His message for the day was that food plants are the key to their presence. In this the Lulworth Skipper has reasonably liberal, if not dire, taste as it can sometimes be found on ragwort. This bitter, obnoxious and injurious yellow-flowering weed – legally notifiable for extermination – can be found in some quantity in no-go parts of the Lulworth Ranges but is hardly to be recommended for the suburban garden. There, we were told, it is not only the purple buddleia that is butterfly friendly but the wall-growing red valerian and a variety of daisies and herbs. It is the closest that many of us will ever come to having our own corner of another county that is forever Lulworth.

Above: *Mollusc carvings by sculptor Peter Randall-Page (right), being inserted into Lulworth walls in a project by Common Ground in the 1980s.*

Right: *'An Ali Baba jar, a cheerful, gigantic, red wasps' nest,' was how Roland Gant described the remains of the limekiln in the cliff at Lulworth Cove. Photographed by Colin Graham in 1983.*

SUBSCRIBERS

Alan and Roza Aldridge, Swanage, Dorset

Lindsey J. Alexander, Stair Hole Cottage, Lulworth Cove, Dorset

Mervyn C. Allen, Sturminster Newton, Dorset

Tim and Sue Armstead, Churchfield House, West Lulworth, Dorset

Colin and Liz Baker, Wool, Dorset

Kim Barr, Lulworth, Dorset

Irvine Barton, West Lulworth, Dorset

Richard, Mandy, Emma-Jay, Charlotte and Matthew Best, Studland, Dorset

John L. Bonney, Poynton, Cheshire

Ronald E. Boswell, Looe, Cornwall

Rosemary Brooker (née Summers)

Rita and Leonard Burden, Winterbourne Zelston

Michael Burge and Emma Parker-Drake, Swanage, Dorset

Richard Burleigh, Charmouth, Dorset

Dawn Buttivant, Uxbridge, Middlesex

Merle and Bob Chacksfield, Swanage, Dorset

Anne and Eddie Clegg, Lancashire

Ronald Charles Cox, Lulworth, Dorset

Paul and Janie Davies, Watford, Hertfordshire

Mr G.W. Dye, Swanage, Dorset

Beryl M. Edey, Wareham, Dorset

Antony J. Eves, West Lulworth, Dorset

Mr and Mrs C. Farley, West Lulworth, Dorset

Christopher G. Finch, Redbourn, Hertfordshire

Lisa Firmstone, Lulworth Cove, Dorset

Tim Firmstone, Lulworth Cove, Dorset

Karen Firmstone, Lulworth Cove, Dorset

Ronald M. Ford, Wareham, Dorset

Mrs T. Forster, Weymouth, Dorset

Alan and Sonia Fynn, Chagford, Devon

Janet Garnish, Wareham, Dorset

T. and J. Gilbert, Wool, Dorset

Delma C. Gomes, Ealing, London

David and Sheila Griffiths, Sandbanks

Noreen G. Hall, East Lulworth

Dorothy Hall, East Lulworth, Dorset

P.J. Halliday, West Lulworth, Dorset

Dr M.J. Halsall

Andrew Hawkes, Poole, Dorset

Grayham and Carol Hemsley, Botany Farm House

Dr and Mrs V.W. Hetreed, Coombe Keynes, Dorset

Bob and Lynn Heydon, The Nest, Main Road, West Lulworth, Dorset

Ms Celia A. Hill, Staines, Middlesex

Rob and Anna Jackson MsRCVS, East Lulworth, Dorset

Judith Jesty, East Lulworth, Dorset

Mrs Mary E. Johnson, Wareham, Dorset

Ken Jones, Dorchester, Dorset

Dennis Jones, Sunnyside, West Lulworth, Dorset

Peter T. Keay, Lulworth, Dorset

Janet B.M. Kelly

Rebecca Helen and Timothy Robert Kennett, Lulworth Castle

Ian and Sarah King, Old Coulsdon, Surrey

Mr and Mrs P. Kirby, Weymouth, Dorset

Norman Langford, Wool, Dorset

Hazel G. Luxford, Woodlands, Hampshire

Heather Maguire, Lulworth, Dorset

Erica Manthorpe (née Spavins), born 1933 West Lulworth

David Manuel, Lulworth, Dorset

Mr Robert and Mrs Teresa Lucy Matthews Giles, Lulworth, Dorset

John McGoldrick, Bovington, Dorset

Alison McKay, Lulworth, Dorset

Doreen and Jim McKenzie, Wareham, Dorset

Ian Methven

James E. Miller, Lulworth Cove, Dorset

David Mitchell, Coastguard Station Officer, Lulworth

Peter Morris, Wool, Dorset

Peter C. Morton, Wool, Dorset

Marion M. Moss, Bournemouth, Dorset

J.G. Naish, Wool, Wareham, Dorset

Mr Trevor O'Sullivan

Stephen T.J. Pack, West Lulworth, Dorset

John and Amanda Peters, Maidenhead, Berkshire

Jon Phillips, The Old Malthouse, Dorset

Nigel Pietrzyba and Lesley Thorpe, Taplow, Berkshire

Mr G.R. Porter, Langton Matravers, Swanage, Dorset

Gary and Karen Prescott, Swanage, Dorset

Charlotte Ranger

Jan S. Ravensdale, Lulworth, Dorset

Richard T. Riding

Mr and Mrs H.W. Riggs, East Lulworth, 1960–2000

Nigel S.J. Selby, East Holme, Dorset

Steve and Rosemary Smith, Wool, Dorset

Carol Smith, Wool, Dorset

Mr and Mrs Andrew Thorpe, Ventnor, Isle of Wight

John F.W. Walling, Newton Abbot, Devon

Jonathan and Susie Walsh, Broadmayne, Dorset

John G. Way, Wool, Dorset

West Lulworth C of E First School,

Anne E. White, Lulworth, Dorset

Annie and Bill Whittle, Lulworth, Dorset

Edward L. Williams, Wool, Dorset

Debra Woodward (née Hall), East Lulworth

Titles from the Series

The Book of Addiscombe • Various
The Book of Addiscombe, Vol. II • Various
The Book of Bampton • Caroline Seward
The Book of Barnstaple • Avril Stone
Book of Bickington • Stuart Hands
Blandford Forum: A Millennium Portrait • Various
The Book of Bridestowe • R. Cann
The Book of Brixham • Frank Pearce
The Book of Buckland Monachorum & Yelverton • Hemery
The Book of Carshalton • Stella Wilks
The Parish Book of Cerne Abbas • Vale & Vale
The Book of Chagford • Ian Rice
The Book of Chittlehamholt with
Warkleigh & Satterleigh • Richard Lethbridge
The Book of Chittlehampton • Various
The Book of Colney Heath • Bryan Lilley
The Book of Constantine • Moore & Trethowan
The Book of Cornwood & Lutton • Various
The Book of Creech St Michael • June Small
The Book of Cullompton • Various
The Book of Dawlish • Frank Pearce
The Book of Dulverton, Brushford,
Bury & Exebridge • Various
The Book of Dunster • Hilary Binding
The Ellacombe Book • Sydney R. Langmead
The Book of Exmouth • W.H. Pascoe
The Book of Grampound with Creed • Bane & Oliver
The Book of Hayling Island & Langstone • Rogers
The Book of Helston • Jenkin with Carter
The Book of Hemyock • Clist & Dracott
The Book of Hethersett • Various
The Book of High Bickington • Avril Stone
The Book of Ilsington • Dick Wills
The Book of Lamerton • Ann Cole & Friends
Lanner, A Cornish Mining Parish • Scharron Schwartz &
Roger Parker
The Book of Leigh & Bransford • Various
The Book of Litcham with Lexham & Mileham • Various
The Book of Loddiswell • Various
The Book of Lulworth • Rodney Legg
The Book of Lustleigh • Joe Crowdy
The Book of Manaton • Various
The Book of Markyate • Various
The Book of Mawnan • Various
The Book of Meavy • Pauline Hemery
The Book of Minehead with Alcombe • Binding & Stevens
The Book of Morchard Bishop • Jeff Kingaby
The Book of Newdigate • John Callcut
The Book of Northlew with Ashbury • Various
The Book of North Newton • Robins & Robins
The Book of North Tawton • Various
The Book of Okehampton • Radford & Radford
The Book of Paignton • Frank Pearce
The Book of Penge, Anerley & Crystal Palace • Various
The Book of Peter Tavy with Cudlipptown • Various
The Book of Pimperne • Jean Coull
The Book of Plymtree • Tony Eames
The Book of Porlock • Denis Corner
Postbridge – The Heart of Dartmoor • Reg Bellamy
The Book of Priddy • Various
The Book of Rattery • Various
The Book of Silverton • Various

The Book of South Molton • Various
The Book of South Stoke • Various
South Tawton & South Zeal with Sticklepath • Radfords
The Book of Sparkwell with Hemerdon & Lee Mill • Pam James
The Book of Staverton • Pete Lavis
The Book of Stithians • Various
The Book of Studland • Rodney Legg
The Book of Swanage • Rodney Legg
The Book of Torbay • Frank Pearce
Uncle Tom Cobley & All: Widecombe-in-the-Moor • Stephen
Woods
The Book of Watchet • Compiled by David Banks
The Book of West Huntspill • Various
Widecombe-in-the-Moor • Stephen Woods
The Book of Williton • Michael Williams
Woodbury: The Twentieth Century Revisited • Roger Stokes
The Book of Woolmer Green • Various

Forthcoming

The Book of Bakewell • Various
The Book of Barnstaple, Vol. II • Avril Stone
The Book of Brampford • Various
The Book of Breage & Gurmoe • Stephen Polglase
The Book of the Bedwyns • Various
The Book of Bideford • Peter Christie
The Book of Bridport • Rodney Legg
The Book of Buckfastleigh • Sandra Coleman
The Book of Carharrack • Various
The Book of Castleton • Geoff Hill
The Book of Edale • Gordon Miller
The Book of Kingskerswell • Various
The Book of Lostwithiel • Barbara Frasier
The Book of Lydford • Barbara Weeks
The Book of Lyme Regis • Rodney Legg
The Book of Nether Stowey • Various
The Book of Nynehead • Various
The Book of Princetown • Dr Gardner-Thorpe
The Book of St Day • Various
The Book of Sampford Courtenay
with Honeychurch • Stephanie Pouya
The Book of Sculthorpe • Garry Windeler
The Book of Sherborne • Rodney Legg
The Book of Southbourne • Rodney Legg
The Book of Tavistock • Gerry Woodcock
The Book of Thorley • Various
The Book of Tiverton • Mike Sampson
The Book of West Lavington • Various
The Book of Witheridge • Various
The Book of Withycombe • Chris Boyles

For details of any of the above titles or if you are
interested in writing your own history, please contact:
Commissioning Editor Community Histories, Halsgrove
House, Lower Moor Way, Tiverton Business Park,
Tiverton, Devon EX16 6SS, England;
email: naomic@halsgrove.com

In order to include as many historic photographs as
possible in this volume, a printed index is not included.
However, the Community History Series is indexed by
Genuki. For further information and indexes to
volumes in the series, please visit:
http://www.cs.ncl.uk/genuki/DEV/indexingproject.html